The Farm on the Wall

Carol Winkler Kotsch

The Farm on the Wall
© 2019 Carol Winkler Kotsch

All rights reserved. No part of this publication may be reproduced, distributed, or transmitted in any form or by any means, without prior written permission of the publisher.

Published by Carol Kotsch
Wichita, KS

Kari Ludes, Cover Art
kraelud@gmail.com

Curtis Becker, Cover Design/Interior Layout/Project Management
curtisbeckerbooks.com
curtis@curtisbeckerbooks.com

ISBN: 978-0-578-55942-1

For my daughters, who wondered what it was like when I was growing up—

For Dad and Uncle Lowell who told stories and answered questions—

In memory of my mother, who was pretty sure I might write something, someday.

Thanks are due to Betty Zajkowski, Leo Oliva, Steve Jansen, and my husband. Their careful proofreading and helpful suggestions greatly improved my story.

"The first things we knew must always be the most familiar...They are the closest, the ones we have known longest. We walk away to other things in the distance, things that were once far off to us. These first things never were far off, and can never be left at a distance. We think we are walking away from them, and wherever we go we carry them with us, without knowing it, and when we return to them everything else recedes to its distance again."

-Eleanor Farjeon, *Kaleidoscope*

Table of Contents

Chapter 1	The Farm on the Wall	1
Chapter 2	Land Boom in the Great American Desert	7
Chapter 3	Taking a Gamble	19
Chapter 4	Starting from Scratch	33
Chapter 5	The Great War, the Flu, and a Dare	41
Chapter 6	To Kansas from the South	51
Chapter 7	The Family Begins to Grow	63
Chapter 8	Harvesting Wheat and Dust	71
Chapter 9	Mining Boom and Bust	85
Chapter 10	Another Generation Begins	99
Chapter 11	Kitchen Table	109
Chapter 12	The Four Seasons of Growing Wheat	121
Chapter 13	From Heat and Dust to Floods and Blizzards	129
Chapter 14	Milk, Beef, and Pork	139
Chapter 15	Horses Return to the Farm	151
Chapter 16	Raising Chickens and Picking Vegetables	161
Chapter 17	Up and Down the Hill	169
Chapter 18	Off to School by Horse and Bus	185
Chapter 19	The Generations After	197

1

The Farm on the Wall

The black and white aerial photograph of the farm that now hangs on our living room wall was taken late in 1955. You can see the tiny figure of my father—your grandfather—standing just to the east of the long shed where the combine was stored after each harvest. He told me he remembered watching a plane fly over, and wondered why it was swooping so low. The answer came a week or two later when a salesman appeared at the farmhouse up the hill where my newlywed mother and father had moved when Dad's aunt and uncle left it empty to retire in Dodge City.

    He was a representative of Photo-Plane Litho Printers, he declared, an aerial photography company based in Boulder, Colorado. Then he pulled out a photo of the farm and asked Dad if he might be related to the folks living on the farm down the hill. He had shown them the picture, the salesman said, but my cautious grandparents—your great-grandparents—who had endured the Depression and drought, and other hard times, considered it an unnecessary luxury. *They wouldn't buy it*, he continued, *and it*

Carol Winkler Kotsch

just seems a shame. It's a good picture, something your family will treasure for years. Would you be interested?

Dad thought long and hard. He and Mom were just starting out and the asking price of $15 would take some doing. He looked at the picture again for a long moment and bought it. That Christmas he and Mom gave it to his parents. Years later, whenever my grandmother couldn't find my grandfather around their house or back yard in Dodge City, she knew he would be in the bedroom, standing before that photograph and staring at the farm he and his father and brothers had created and sweated over.

Grandpa—your grandpa's father—pointed out the picture to me once when I was small. *Do you know where that is?* he asked, pointing to the farm on the wall. I stared at the picture in confusion. I thought I knew what it was, but the buildings looked distorted and odd; I doubt I had ever seen an aerial photo before. And then I recognized the barn and the house, and it fell into place. Everything was the same, except the white picket fence surrounding the house was gone, and I could tell Dad had made some additions to the corrals.

From time to time while growing up, I would duck into my grandparents' bedroom in Dodge City and stare at the picture. The farm where I lived, and the farm on the wall stayed much the same for many years, but after a while I started noticing other changes. And then I was in high school and off to college; I married and started a family, and visits to my grandfather were less frequent. His health declined and he moved into the Bethel Home in Montezuma. As he faded away, his mind reverted to the days on the farm before my father married. He no longer understood who I was, but he enjoyed meeting you, Jackie, though he couldn't understand who you were, either. *It's been a long time since I held a baby*, he said in a thin voice. I didn't see the farm on the wall again until after his death.

It came quietly and gently on February 28, 1991; he was 95 and the last of his siblings. We buried him two days later on the second of March, a bitter, bitter cold day—the temperature was 27 degrees and the 23 mile-per-hour north wind made it feel like

The Farm on the Wall

12. You girls were very small—Laura had just turned three years and Jackie eight months. We left you, Laura, with family friends while we went to Dodge City for the funeral, but Jackie came with us. After the funeral we drove to Fairview Cemetery, just a couple of miles east of Montezuma. The short, dark green winter wheat in the fields surrounding the cemetery was still dormant. Jackie and I sat inside the car wrapped in blankets while everyone else was gathered around the gravesite.

While we huddled together, I thought about the last time I had been to Fairview for a funeral; it was for my grandmother—your grandpa's mother—in 1974. It took place on the last day of April, and it was a beautiful spring day, calm and clear. The wheat was tall and heading out. You could see almost to Cimarron, over fifteen miles away. Though Grandma and Grandpa had retired to Dodge in 1960, they had lived in the community for many years, and their neighbors did not forget. There must have been 50 and more cars parked on either side of the cemetery gates.

I remember the pastor finished the final prayer, and the coffin was lowered. My grandfather's knees began to buckle, and Dad and Uncle Lowell grabbed his arms to steady him. He recovered, but sat down, and then a steady line of mourners and neighbors began to offer condolences.

As folks began to drift away, or break up into smaller groups, I wandered around the headstones, looking at names I had heard all my life: Algrim, Bargar, Bindley, Blackwelder, Dern, Fry, Gamble, Hargett, Hedlund, Hendrickson, Jacques, Markel, McCalmont, Monninger, Robertson, Ullom, Wade, and my own great-grandparents, O. R. and Mary Winkler. Now my grandmother was there, buried next to her first child, a son who had died shortly after birth.

Since it was so cold, the graveside service for Grandpa was very short; there was no lingering with neighbors and friends at the cemetery. We picked you up, Laura, and gathered with the rest of the family at the café in Montezuma. In just a few years we would all be gathered again at Fairview to bury my mother—your grandmother. This time it would be a warm day in June and the

Carol Winkler Kotsch

wheat was gold and ready to cut. The line of cars at the cemetery was long once again. Neighbors helped Dad finish the harvest, and you two rode in the combine.

When we returned home after Grandpa's funeral, I wondered what would happen to the farm on the wall. My querulous aunt had inherited the house in Dodge City and had possession of all the contents. Dad spoke to her, and she agreed to relinquish the photo, along with a few other odds and ends—some china and old silverware. I stored away the china—it belonged to Grandma's family, the Ethertons—and displayed the silverware in the old brown teapot I once used to make iced tea in during harvest. The picture of the farm I took and hung next to my arrowheads and the picture of the one-room school Dad and Uncle Lowell attended.

Now I look at the photograph where it hangs on the wall of our house, and stare at the unchanging farm in southwest Kansas where I grew up. I have tried to track down Photo-Plane Litho Printers, but no record exists of them at the state level, and neither the Boulder Public Library nor the Denver Public Library could find any trace of them. *Aerial photo companies come and go*, the owner of a Denver aerial photo company told me. His company had been in business since 1948, and he had never heard of them.

The farm in the picture looks very much as it did during the 1930s, when your grandpa was a boy. There's the house, of course, forever surrounded by the neat, white picket fence. My great-grandpa and his sons built it in 1916. The window closest to the smaller cedar tree was mine, and it looked out to the south.

The cylinder next to the windmill is the supply tank that we always kept topped with water. There used to be a little patch of rhubarb that grew at its base. The little square white building is the milk house where Grandpa and Uncle stored the milk to keep it cool before it was picked up. The garden is just to the left of the supply tank so it could be easily watered. More rhubarb lined the garden along the south side next to the fence, and a bed of asparagus was on the west end.

A small cowshed is on the other side of the garden, and the

little building on the extreme west edge is the old forge, where Uncle used to make horseshoes. After the horses were gone from the farm, he turned to repairing the machinery. Grandpa handled the financial part of the farm, said Dad, while Uncle took care of tractors and trucks.

The building with the large white sliding door that stands catty-corner to the house is the granary. During harvest, Grandpa and Uncle backed the trucks in and unloaded the wheat by hand, scoop by scoop, to store against a better price. Dad used to keep seed wheat in there, but in time the bins were left empty. We stored the saddles and bridles for the horses in them, and Dad kept his doctoring supplies for the cattle in a corner, along with the branding iron. There were large coils of barb wire piled in the back that looked tempting to climb on, but were too sharp and prickly to attempt.

The largest building is the barn—I spent many, many hours there. The outer door is open, so you can see the half-door, a Dutch door, Dad called it; it let air circulate in the barn for the cows. Several times Grandpa and Dad had to make a leap over that half-door when one of the milk cows didn't want them around her new-born calf. Dad discovered he could jump pretty high with an angry cow behind him.

The white building is the chicken house. A laying flock was once kept there, and I can remember rows of nesting boxes on one side. Later, it was converted to a workshop and garage. On the east side of the picture is the long shed that held plows and other implements, and a small grain bin. Next to that you can see a small workshop that smelled of grease and was full of tools I didn't recognize. Last of all, the tiny brooder house where baby chicks were raised.

I explored every silent building, disturbing the spiders as I poked around in the dust. Each one was as familiar to me as the back of my hand. Only the barn is still standing on the farm where I spent my first eighteen years, but I can close my eyes and see it, and hear it, and smell it, as clearly as though it was just down the road, waiting for me to come back and take up my long-neglected chores. It grew and changed and vanished in bits and pieces over the years while I was growing up, as new methods of farming and more efficient equipment meant that old tools and buildings had outlived their usefulness.

One by one they were torn down. I helped toss the battered bricks of the milk house into the pickup truck to be hauled off to the dump, and dragged the faded white picket fence over to a bonfire, and watched as the barn up the hill was leveled off and plowed over, and the forge was cleaned out and demolished. The old farmhouse itself was sold and moved away to Wilroads Gardens, a little town just southeast of Dodge City, in 1977. The original half section from 1910 became two sections by the time my father retired in 1998, and my parents added new structures over the years, and built a new house, but it is the farm I grew up with that I remember best. The farmyard is empty now, though, and buffalo grass is reclaiming the gravel circle where trucks and tractors and pickups once made their daily rounds.

As I followed Dad around the farm, or up the hill to check the well, I listened to stories about the buildings and the land, and the people who lived there. Some of them I heard many times over the years, others in bits and pieces from neighbors that I had to put together later. It seemed at the time I heard them that the life I knew would go on forever and ever amen, but as I watched people pass on, and buildings decay and fall and be forgotten, I realized the same would happen to the stories I had heard, events that shaped my family, and the farm, and me.

2

Land Boom in the Great American Desert

The half-section of land in Gray County, Kansas, where my grandfather and father would one day grow wheat and raise cattle, was part of what was once known as the "Great American Desert," in the nineteenth century. The lack of trees and water made it unsuitable for farming, according to the thought of the day. The southwest corner of the state was the last to be developed; the lusher eastern half had been mostly settled before the Civil War era. The Homestead Act of 1862, plus later land acts, such as Timber Culture Act of 1873, attracted more would-be farmers. Planting groves of trees on the empty plains would improve the weather and bring more rain, it was believed, and the Timber Act would give settlers an additional 160 acres for planting 40 acres to timber. Still, settlement was slow.

But once the Indians had been cleared out after the Red River Wars in the Texas Panhandle in 1875[1] and were no longer terrorizing the Texas-Oklahoma-Kansas region, then investors began buying up blocks of land in southwest Kansas. A land boom began during the 1880s, and the area was swept by promoters seeking to build cities to rival those of the East.[2]

Gray County was created in 1881, but the boundaries changed several times, as well as the name, until 1887, when it was finally organized. It was named for Alfred Gray, a transplanted New Yorker who served during the Civil War, and later became the Secretary of the Kansas Board of Agriculture. He died of tuberculosis in 1880, just as the boom was beginning.

Initially, there were three towns: Cimarron, Ingalls, and Montezuma. The first was Montezuma, platted by a group of Kansas businessmen—the Western Kansas Town and Land Company—who purchased title to the land in 1886, hoping to make it into a business and agricultural trading empire. The exotic name "was so completely associated with gold that Americans used it to refer to money," and was probably chosen to lure investors; the streets boasted equally exotic and unpronounceable names.[3]

The Dodge City Times noted on April 28, 1887, that "Montezuma will soon enjoy a name as memoriable [sic] as its ancient namesake." A corner business lot went for $200, and residential lots for $30 and $50. A post office made it official that same year. Soon, nearly 300 optimistic citizens and farmers had moved in; before long, Montezuma reveled in a doctor and a newspaper.[4]

It also boasted an "electrical well." "The new town of Montezuma is deeply interested in the extraordinary phenomenon of an electrical well, the water of which appears to have extraordinary curative powers." Dr. T.J. Wheeler, a member of the Western Kansas Town and Land Company, was the owner of the Hotel Montezuma where the newly-dug well was located. Witnesses claimed that "an electrical flame...gathers every night at the top of the pump rod" and "it gives a strong buzzing sound."[5]

The buzzing electrical flames evidently imparted healing properties to the water. Mrs. Wheeler claimed to have been cured of her chronic rheumatism, and "can ascribe no other cause than use of the water from the electrical well." Other similar sufferers reported experiencing relief.[6]

Indeed, investors looked for any angle to attract buyers. A few years later, in 1890, a Chicago-based company, The Arkansas Valley Sanitarium Association, decided to take advantage of "the dry bracing air," "the delectable climate," and the moderate altitude.[7] It purchased 500 acres of "valuable land" in Cimarron and turned the hotel into a "recuperating station"[8] for those suffering from "pulmonic and bronchial maladies." The sanitarium did not last long, and by the 1900s was turned back into a hotel.

Reports of the "healing qualities of the wonderful climate in Western Kansas" appeared in eastern magazines and newspapers, and caught the eye of James A. Luther, who lived in Indiana. He had contracted tuberculosis, and in 1884 arbitrarily picked Cimarron by "dividing his total resources by the rate per mile for railroad tickets"[9] and moved his family there. He started a real estate business and wrote and urged his brother, F. M., to join him and get rich quick. "Dad fell for it," his son, Lester, later recorded.[10]

One of a family of 13, Francis Marion Luther was born in Indiana in 1854. He married Camilla Duty in 1880 and moved to Mantoon, Illinois, where he took a job with the railroad. His first son, Forrest, was born there in 1883, and there the family might have remained had it not been for James's letter. F.M. moved his wife and three children out west in February, 1886, and joined his brother's business. Two weeks later, a blizzard struck. A week of heavy snow forced some homesteaders to burn their furniture to stay warm, and thousands of cattle drifted with the storm and died. After the storm was over, F.M. wanted to take his family back east, but had only $14 in his pocket—not enough for train tickets.[11]

Luther Brothers, Real Estate Brokers, didn't last very long, however, for it became F.M. Luther in 1887.[12] James moved to Caldwell, Missouri, where he died in 1896, and F.M. seems to have run the business on his own until his sons were old enough to join him. Despite the inauspicious start, he was convinced of the area's potential, and became a fixture in the development of the region. "F.M. Luther, of Cimarron, one of the original Luther's

[sic] and a hustling real estate man, is here on business," noted *The Great Bend Weekly Tribune* on August 20, 1909.

A year after F. M.'s arrival, Cimarron was declared the temporary seat of the newly-organized Gray County, a title that the other two towns, Ingalls and Montezuma, hoped to win permanently. That would have to wait until the October 31 election of the same year. Ingalls and Cimarron had the advantage of sitting on the Santa Fe railroad; Montezuma, however, sat about eighteen miles south of the line and had no such attraction to encourage further growth.[13]

Enter Asa T. Soule, an ambitious patent-medicine millionaire and entrepreneur from New York who was not content with his millions from the sale of "Soule's Hop Bitters, The Invalid's Friend and Hope." He had purchased a baseball team, and backed boat races in order to add to his prestige, but each venture ended in scandal.[14] Learning of cheap land for sale in Kansas, Soule began to dream of his own agricultural empire by using the Arkansas River as a source of irrigation that would surely make the dry, but fertile southwest corner flourish.

Since 1883, he had been involved in financing the Eureka Irrigating Canal Company. With its start at Ingalls, the canal was planned to be over 90 miles long, following a ridge north of the Arkansas River, and the Santa Fe railroad track, and ending at Coon Creek, forty-five miles east of Spearville.[15] Soule poured in about $800,000 of his money to finance the construction of the canal, which provided work for hundreds of men during 1884-85.[16] Using five ditching machines, each pulled by twelve horses, construction gangs crept along at the rate of two miles a week.[17]

It was to Soule's advantage to have the Gray County seat located in Ingalls, which he envisioned as the center of his empire. In an attempt to sway voters for the upcoming election in October 1887, he dangled the bribe of a railroad before Montezuma and Ensign, if the inhabitants of those towns would vote for Ingalls as the Gray County seat. Despite Soule's attempt to purchase the election by distributing checks for a hundred dollars and more, and some ballot-stuffing, both Cimarron and Ingalls claimed the victory.[18] The dispute went to the Kansas Supreme Court which ruled for Ingalls, and county records were transferred there in 1888.

The town of Montezuma was rewarded after the election. Thirty-five miles of track were laid, and named the Dodge City, Montezuma, and Trinidad Line. Part of the Arkansas, Kansas & Colorado Railroad and operated by the Chicago, Rock Island & Pacific line, it was intended to haul wheat to market and bring back coal from Colorado, but it never reached west of Montezuma.[19] For eight years trains shuttled back and forth from Montezuma to Dodge City, but never at a profit to Soule.[20]

While Soule was involved with building his railroad and canal, Cimarron continued to press its case. In the semi-arid region of southwest Kansas, where the whims of the weather determined a good harvest, and economic prosperity was often on a knife-edge, being named the county seat meant life or death for a small community. More rulings and elections followed, alternating in favor of one town to the other, with the records going back and forth, and eventually ending up in Cimarron, though Ingalls was the official seat.

Ingalls officials were determined to return the records to their rightful place. With the backing of Soule, a group of hired thugs from Dodge City that included Bat Masterson's brother Jim, drove a wagon to Cimarron in January of 1889. Flashing their guns at the town clerk, they demanded he turn over the remaining county papers. While the clerk delayed, word of the attempted seizure got around, and as the hired guns loaded the wagon with what they could grab, they found themselves surrounded by the men of Cimarron. Guns were drawn and shots were fired, though later, no one could say for certain who had fired first.

F.M. Luther himself was among the Cimarron defenders, at one point chasing an Ingalls man around and around a building. When Luther paused to get off a shot at the invader, his revolver jammed. The Ingalls man continued running around the building, and began chasing Luther instead, who managed to hide and save himself. Afterwards, he found a bullet hole through his derby hat, and a lock of hair clipped off.[21]

Several were wounded on both sides, and one man—J.W. English of Cimarron—was killed. Some of the "Ingalls" men—including Jim Masterson—holed up inside the temporary Cimarron courthouse while the rest dashed back to Ingalls with the county papers.[22]

Dad told me about the battle one day when we were leaving Cimarron after buying some tractor parts. He pointed out the old courthouse—an old-fashioned storefront just south of Clark's Drugstore where we used to go for ice cream sodas. It was originally built as a department store in 1880, and leased to the county later. The modern courthouse was built just a few blocks to the south in 1927.

I looked around in disbelief at the small downtown with its one stoplight, and a couple of law-abiding pedestrians strolling down the streets. *A gunfight—here—in Gray County?* I couldn't imagine the local farmers I saw out in the fields on their tractors, or drinking coffee at the drugstore joining a mob and shooting guns. *Yes*, said Dad, *they were that desperate to get the county seat awarded to them.*

When the shooting was over and the invaders had surrendered, the sheriff, an Ingalls man himself, wired Governor John Martin that he could not suppress the riot and requested a company of militia.[23] The national guardsmen kept order, and the event made the pages of *The New York Tribune*.[24]

On January 14, 1889, the *St. Louis Dispatch* recorded

> A company of militia has arrived at Cimarron, Kan., where the riot occurred Saturday and all is now quiet there. A warrant has been sworn out against R. H. Herrington, Ace Herrington, Hugh Hudson, W. J. Dixon, O. J. Dixon, J. C. Bauer, Ellis Garten, Harry Brice, Frank Luther, Joe Newport, and J. M. Weeks, charging them with assault to kill, and all of them have been arrested. The men are those who resisted the Ingalls crowd in taking away the records.

The Kansas Supreme Court declared in favor of Ingalls. The shooting was over, but "the Stevens and Gray county [sic] seat wars cost the state of Kansas nearly $10,000.[25] It appeared that Soule had been victorious. Soule, however, returned to Rochester, New York, not long after; he died barely a year later, in January, 1890.[26] The *Semi-Weekly Interior Journal* of Stanford, Kentucky, dryly remarked, "Asa Soule, who made $2,000,000 out of hop bitters, has gone where no bitters are needed. He didn't take a cent with him."[27]

The canal, which he had sold to other speculators for $1,000,000, was never finished. Like the 30 other similar irrigation canal projects in the area, it succumbed to drought.[28] A few years later, in 1908, new investors tried again with two centrifugal pumps, each weighing 15 tons. Though they could pump 30,000 gallons of water a minute, the sandy soil and the lack of dependable rainfall again defeated them.

Ironically, the steam-powered pumps were buried in in mud and silt from a disastrous flood that reached far downstream from Pueblo, Colorado. Over six inches of rain fell in just a few hours north and west of Pueblo in early June of 1921, and the Arkansas River quickly rose to over 15 feet. Freight cars and even entire buildings were swept away in an overflow that covered over 300 square miles. As many as 1500 people may have died. By the time the water reached the Ingalls area, most of its force was spent, but a local resident remembered that "we could hear the roar as that gushing water came down through this area. The noise could be heard for several miles."[29]

The 18-feet pumps were forgotten until 1977 when one was dug up and put on display in Ingalls.[30] Mounds of dirt from Soule's excavation lined Highway 50 from Ingalls to Dodge, but over the years they became covered with cactus and yucca. They resembled grass-covered scoops of ice cream to me, and I thought they were just part of the landscape until Dad explained otherwise.

The boom created by Soule as he sprinkled his wealth around the two counties, financing a streetcar system in Dodge City, purchasing the bank and the waterworks, donating land to start a university—Soule College, later St. Mary's of the Plains—and backing the canal project, died off as a drought in the early 1890s dried up the harvests that would sustain his empire.[31] The hundreds of hopeful citizens who had flooded the county seeking agricultural riches began to drift away elsewhere.

The population of Ingalls declined to 100.[32] Cimarron fared a little better, and in an uncontested special election in 1893, the title of county seat was finally and permanently awarded to it. F. M. Luther would become mayor in 1907, and was remembered for replacing the wooden sidewalks with concrete, pushing for the waterworks system to be rebuilt, and having the city take over the electric light plant.[33]

Montezuma's promising start was also ended by the drought, and by the opening of the Cherokee Strip in Oklahoma in 1893, which drained most of its population away.[34] When the railroad closed in 1894, the town was nearly destroyed.[35] The Kansas legislature declared it dead the following year. The rails were taken up and sold off, and the aggrieved farmers took the ties to use as fence posts.[36] The deserted businesses and residences were shipped to Enid, Oklahoma. Only a few hardy settlers remained behind.

Still, Gray County boosters continued to promote the area. "Get in on the ground floor," urged "The Gray Book," a promotional pamphlet published about 1907 by the Gray County Commercial Club in Cimarron, praising the resources of the county. Land in Ford County was selling for $50 to $100 an acre around Dodge City, it pointed out, while in Gray County it was considerably cheaper at $5 to $12.50. Wheat was yielding 30-40 bushels per acre, and the land was good for growing corn, oats, barley, alfalfa, sugar beets, and even fruit trees. Families can make enough money from a flock of 100 hens to keep them in groceries for a year, it declared, and stock could graze or be fed throughout the winter.[37]

It assured readers that 17 to 20 inches of rain was plenty of moisture for farming, if you followed the Campbell system of soil culture, by plowing deeply, and then using the Campbell "subsurface packer" to trap moisture. Hardy Webster Campbell, a homesteader from South Dakota, developed methods for dry-land farming that he believed would reduce evaporation and drifting soil.[38] Farmers worked the soil repeatedly after every shower until a layer of fine particles covered the surface, which supposedly provided a layer of "dust mulch" that would keep the moisture from evaporating.[39] Campbell declared all ground cover should be removed, which actually promoted evaporation and wind erosion, though no one realized it at the time.

Then, some 15 years later, things began to change for the town that had been declared dead. Despite the failure of Soule's enterprise, the Atchison, Topeka and the Santa Fe noticed that the southwest corner of Kansas was similar to the farmland around Amarillo, Texas, where farmers were producing respectable harvests, providing the ATSF with good revenue. The ATSF began to make plans for developing the area west of Dodge City, and bought up some 256,000 acres, intending to sell them to farmers, and in 1912 began to develop a new line running west of Dodge City to the future town of Elkhart, founded in 1913. [40]

On February 16, 1912, *The Liberal Democrat* noted, "Ten cars of mules and grading implements arrived at Dodge City last week, and the first grading camp on the Santa Fe was established eight miles west of Dodge City. The names of Ensign and Montezuma, two new towns, were selected last week. Montezuma will be located on section 24 and 25 in township 28 south and range 29 west."[41]

Montezuma was revived. A new community was laid out about a mile and half north from the old site, and with the assurance of transportation for crops, it slowly began to grow again. The newspaper resumed publishing in 1912, changing the name from *Montezuma News*, to *The Montezuma Chief*, and finally to *The Montezuma Press*. It called itself "A Boosting Little Paper in the Best Little Town in the Best Little County in Kansas," and faithfully recorded all the local news. There was nothing left of the ambitious plans for a YMCA, a race track, four elementary schools, a

Carol Winkler Kotsch

high school, and a college for the original Montezuma, but Dad pointed out the old rail trestle south of town one day when we were picking up tractor parts.⁴²

The drought and opening up of land in Oklahoma during the 1890s had affected Luther's real estate business as well. Homesteaders pulled up and left, and mortgage companies foreclosed. Land sales slacked off, and profits shrank. To compensate, he would buy up some 50 or more quarter sections, and head back east to Illinois, where he would trade them for workhorses, which were scarce in Gray County. F. M. would then ship the horses to Gray County and sell them for $100 to $150 to the local farmers.⁴³

F. M.'s name must have become known around Illinois, for in 1897, C. H. Moore from Clinton, arrived in F. M.'s office to look at land in Kansas and ended up buying 60 quarters after F. M. had shown him around the county.⁴⁴ After that, the business prospered and son Forrest began making trips in his father's stead. He placed advertisements in local papers and put notices around different towns advertising good land for sale in Kansas.

In the spring of 1910, one of those notices appeared in Lockport, Illinois, and caught the eye of my great-grandfather, Otto Reinhold Winkler, a 43-year-old German immigrant living there with his family in a borrowed home. Intrigued, he attended a meeting with his young sons, and listened to Forrest Luther paint a glowing picture of the arable land out in southwest Kansas. It was sure to produce bountiful wheat harvests, and farmers would be able to send their grain to market on the nearby railroad that was coming. The land was flat, Otto learned, which meant erosion wouldn't be a problem, and horses wouldn't exhaust themselves pulling a plow up and down hills.

The "rich black and the warm sandy loam soils of this section are very fertile and productive," F. M. wrote in "Two Stories," a promotional pamphlet he published a year later in 1911. "The principal field crops are wheat, corn, oats, barley, broom corn, milo-maize, kaffir, and sorghum, all raised successfully and successively without irrigation." He went on to add that it was also "admirably adapted to fruit raising," "exceptionally adapted" for cattle raising, and that "the Helpful Hen finds an ideal home in Gray County" and "hogs...afford big profits." As far as water was concerned, "the well-known underflow of the Arkansas river [sic] is the basis of supply," and that Gray County "receives annually from 18 to 22 inches of rainfall."[45]

Otto listened attentively as Forrest described the resources of the area; it sounded almost too good to be true. After thinking it over for several weeks, he decided to make a trip out west to see it himself. In August, he arrived at Cimarron's train depot. From there, he and Forrest traveled cross-country by a team-drawn surrey on the Stage Line, a road which ran southwest from Cimarron to a post office called Wabash, and then to a tiny settlement called Stowe. When the Atchison, Topeka, and Santa Fe Railroad replaced the Santa Fe Trail, it built stage lines from railroad towns to transport mail out into the "hinterland" communities.[46] Stowe and Wabash no longer exist, and the Stage Line was plowed under long ago, but ruts from the Santa Fe Trail wagons are still visible west of Dodge.

F. M. Luther and Sons had been escorting their clients by car since 1904, and boasted five automobiles—and a garage—but the ruts in the road to this particular piece of property may have been too rough and deep for the tires of the day. As they trotted along the Stage Line, Forrest counted and checked the surveyor's posts until they were just a short distance from a piece of land he had in mind to show Otto. It had first been platted in 1887; a representative of the U.S. government sold it that same year to one Lewis R. Burrows for $200. A year later he sold it for $800.

It changed hands many times during the next 22 years, as land speculators tried to make a profit from it, though it was never farmed. F. M. and his son Forrest first acquired it in 1907, and sold it back and forth several times to different investors until July 1910 when it was back under Forrest's name. It was located in Montezuma Township, about three miles north and four and a half miles west of where the town would be resurrected.

Otto found himself looking at a shortgrass prairie that was flat and empty, punctuated by a few slight hills that gently rose and fell to the horizon, ten miles and more in the distance. It was dotted with spiky mounds of yucca—what we always called "soapweeds"—and clumps of brush and prickly-pear cactus. There were no trees, except by the scarce rivers and creeks. The summers were blistering, the winters freezing, and there was a constant south wind. The average rainfall was seventeen inches or so, but it might vary from a scant nine inches one year to an abundant twenty or more the next. Dull green buffalo grass and blue grama grew in the rich soil underfoot, though the buffalo that once grazed there, and the Indians who roamed across the plains hunting them were gone. It seemed a most unlikely place for a middle-aged man in failing health to purchase land.

But with the promise of railroads and good crops, and a town coming back to life, Otto liked what he saw of Gray County. He bought a subscription to the Cimarron newspaper: "O.R. Winkler of Lockport, Illinois, was one of the late additions to the Jacksonian subscription list."[47] He made a down payment of $900 on the south half of section six, township 29 south and range 28 west, on November 27, 1910, and took over an existing mortgage of $1500. Forrest Luther signed the note. The price of the two quarters of land—320 acres—would amount to $4,250, about $13 per acre. The land, though, would remain untouched as he wouldn't return for six years.

3

Taking a Gamble

Otto Reinhold Winkler, your great-great-grandfather, was born October 14, 1867, in the German state of Saxony to a gambler father and his wife. I was about 12 or 13 when Grandpa told me about his father. I knew vaguely that Otto, or O. R., as he was usually called, came from Germany, but nothing about how he ended up in southwest Kansas. I asked about him one day while visiting my grandparents in their Dodge City home. Grandpa could share only a few details with me. The facts have grown blurred and forgotten as one generation has passed the story on to another, and another.

Ernestine Marquitz, O. R.'s mother, tired of her husband Traugott's drinking and gambling, and divorced him. *Some of the children went with their mother*, Grandpa told me, *but my dad, he lived with his father*. With the two younger siblings out of the way—Anna Lydia and Frank Charles—Traugott was free to continue gambling but took the precaution of locking his oldest son in the basement before he went out carousing. Sometimes he was lucky, and O. R. would awake to find his father bent over a wash basin, running his fingers through the coins he'd won, and laughing to himself—Grandpa demonstrated for me, scooping up imaginary money in his hands, and letting it trickle away. Other times Traugott would stumble home with empty pockets, cursing and railing at his luck.

He had a hard life, Grandpa said, and then he stopped for a moment. I remember thinking about our basement. I wasn't afraid to go down there anymore, oh no, but when I was little, it was different. Our old basement was gloomy and damp, made with rough, bare cement. The small narrow windows let in very little light, and the single bare light bulb didn't extend to the cobwebby corners where I could see strange outlines of discarded furniture. The gas furnace made odd clicking noises, and the house creaked as it settled. Of course, I knew there was no one down there, but when I turned my back to go upstairs, I was sure I was being watched.

What would it be like to have my father lock me downstairs for the night? The thought filled me with alarm; I didn't know what it was like to have a family like this. Did Traugott beat his son as well? He probably did, but I cannot now remember if Grandpa actually said so.

Traugott had a brother who lived in Lockport, Illinois, Grandpa continued, and owned a farm. This brother, Frederick Winkler, was O.R.'s uncle, I found out later. Frederick was born in 1826, the third oldest of 15 children; Traugott was born in 1828. Their father, Gottlieb Winkler, was a carpenter, but Frederick was apprenticed as a stone mason at the age of 17. He left Germany in 1852, landing first in New York, and then travelling wherever he could find work as a mason: Philadelphia, Delaware, Pittsburg, Cincinnati, and finally to Lockport in 1855, where he bought a farm. There he married Elizabeth Burkhardt, another German immigrant, in 1859. An account of their 50th wedding anniversary reported that "through hard labor and economy they have gained a good living and raised a large family."[1] Some of this probably spilled over into the letters he sent back to his family in Germany.

The Farm on the Wall

What town did O. R. come from? I interrupted. Grandpa didn't know; if his father had told him, he no longer remembered. *Berlin?* I persisted; it was the only city in Germany that I knew of at the time. Grandpa just shrugged.

I've been putting together the pieces of O. R.'s life for years now, girls, and have made several discoveries along the way, information your grandpa and Uncle Lowell did not know. When I read Frederick's obituary and found he was born in Niederdorf, Saxony, I presumed that O. R. and his family must have come from the same town, as O. R.'s obituary lists his birthplace as Saxony. However, Frederick's descendants say he was born in Gera, and the account of his 50th wedding anniversary makes the same statement. Niederdorf is about 50 miles east of Gera and it seemed reasonable to assume that O.R. came from either of those cities, but I had no evidence. I was resigned to not knowing, but then O. R.'s brother, Frank, provided the answer.

Frank, who was nine years younger than O. R., didn't arrive in the United States until several years after his big brother. He didn't stay in Illinois or move to Kansas, but eventually headed west for California. In 1936, one year after the Social Security Act was passed, Frank filed an application for benefits. For place of birth, he recorded Schmölln, Germany.

Old by American standards, the small city of Schmölln—the current population is about 11,000—dates back to 1066. Located in the Altenburger land district of Thuringia in the former East Germany—part of the old kingdom of Saxony—Schmölln is about 15 miles east of Gera, and 157 miles southwest of Berlin. It was a region that underwent many changes of boundaries and names and rulers as Germany slowly unified not long after O. R. was born. Though Thuringia is famous for the Thuringian and Franconian forests and the Harz Mountains—it's known as the "green heart of Germany"—the Altenburger district is flat and fertile and primarily agricultural; [2] the modern city has added automotive manufacturing, plastics, and metalworking. Johann Sebastian Bach lived in the area for a time, and so did Martin Luther.

It was a hard life, my grandpa repeated, *and my dad, he de-*

cided he would follow his uncle to America for something better. At the age of twelve, he left school—the 1940 census shows he had a seventh grade education—and went to work for a baker. Grandpa simply said that he got up at four in the morning to light the fire in the oven, but didn't tell me any more details that I remember.

O. R. and the other baker's boys—there were likely several—not only lit the fire, but probably cut the wood as well, and pumped the water needed for the day. They may have assisted the baker in preparing the dough in the dough tubs or troughs that had risen overnight, shaping it into individual loaves for a second rising. While those loaves were baking in the now-hot oven, they set to work on a second round.

When the day's baking was done, it was time to start a new batch of dough to rise overnight. The flour and water and yeast were mixed in the dough tubs, and the laborious task of kneading began. There had been mechanical kneading machines in use since the previous century, but they didn't really come into use commercially until to the late 1800s. O. R. may not have been big or strong enough to lift and pummel the heavy masses of dough, but he was likely saddled with cleaning the bakery and washing all of the baking utensils, and making sure everything was ready for the next day. Then it was time to go home to eat and sleep before another early rising. He probably hid part of his pay from his father.

After two years, O. R. decided he had enough money to book passage on an immigrant ship to America, where surely life would be much better. He did not know it, but he would exchange the heat of the bread ovens for something much hotter. Grandpa did not tell me what port O. R. went to—Bremen or Hamburg—or how he got there. Both are several hundred miles from Schmölln, much too far to walk. Though Germany was not officially united until 1871, the railroad system had connected the country in the 1840s.[3] German immigration, driven mostly by economic reasons, subsequently jumped from 7,729 from 1820-30, to 152,454 from 1831-40. It hit a peak of 1,452,970 from 1881-1890.[4]

The Farm on the Wall

As crowds from within Germany and the surrounding countries flocked toward the ports of Bremen and Hamburg, businesses realized there was money to be made from the passing emigrants; others saw them as a cultural threat and spreading disease. "German benevolent groups," worried about their well-being, worked with the railroads to persuade them to offer reduced rates—and reduced comfort—in special emigrant cars, where they were locked in and isolated from regular passengers.[5] Travel agents began advertising their transportation services to overseas ports in the local newspapers.[6]

When O. R. arrived at Bremen—or Hamburg—he pulled out his carefully hoarded money for a ticket and discovered that he didn't have enough. Grandpa told me some official took pity on him, and let O. R. board in exchange for working off the rest of what he owed. He would spend the voyage across the Atlantic mucking out the manure in the hold where cattle were kept to provide fresh milk for the first class passengers, despite the valuable space that was taken up for their feed; they were also apt to break a leg during a storm. Sometimes even pigs and chickens were carried as well.[7]

As I listened to my grandpa's story about his father, I realized in astonishment this was right out of my history book at school, and that it had actually happened in my own family. *What was it like on the ship?* I asked Grandpa. He paused again, shook his head, and said you couldn't imagine it. It seemed simple enough to me at that age, and I didn't give much thought to what it had been like for O. R., until I was much older and could research it for myself.

Third class passengers like O. R. journeyed in steerage, the bottom of the ship, which was about perhaps about six to eight feet in height, and dark and unventilated. Along with up to 1000 other fortune-seeking travelers, he slept on a straw-stuffed mattress in one of the hard, wooden bunks that lined steerage in rows from top to bottom. Some ships might provide a thin blanket; these were so filthy at the end of the voyage, that it was cheaper for the passengers to carry them off than it was for the ship to have them cleaned.[8] There were separate "dormitories" for men, women, families, and for married women traveling with children, but without husbands.[9] Perhaps O.R. slept with the first group.

A line of buckets behind a curtain served as toilets for several hundred people, and some ships might provide a washroom for men and women where they could clean hands and face with saltwater, but most passengers were not able to wash themselves or their clothing. Lice spread easily in such crowded, unsanitary living conditions, and outbreaks of ship-fever—typhus—were common. On some ships, the drinking water was contaminated, and passengers died of cholera, sometimes so many that immigrant ships were called "floating coffins" by the newspapers of the day.

The quality of the food was a common complaint of passengers. Cheap and carelessly prepared, it consisted mainly of fish and bread and soup, with perhaps some vegetables or stewed fruit. As they lined up in the cafeteria rooms, those in steerage were expected to provide their own plates, cups, and utensils, though there was no place to wash them.[10] Some immigrants, though, were so sea-sick they could not eat for the entire voyage.

Passengers might also be set upon by fellow travelers. Petty theft was a problem, and tempers flared in the cramped quarters, sometimes as a result of ethnic differences. Women and girls had to fight off advances from other passengers, and the ship's crew as well. Once they were settled in, there was nothing to do, unless someone had brought cards or a musical instrument.[11] They could walk above deck on some ships, but the promenade might be very limited.[12]

It took O. R. six weeks to cross, I remember Grandpa telling me, though most passages by this time took place on quicker steam ships, and lasted about 10-12 days.[13] He arrived in New York City in 1882, one of the nearly 800,000 who came that year.[14] When he disembarked, he took with him whatever few possessions he had carried from Germany, as well as a stink that permeated his clothes and belongings, a smell composed of unwashed bodies, bilge water, vomit, excrement, and stale food. It was an odor unique to steerage passengers, and one that might take a year to fade.[15]

Such wretched, uncomfortable, sometimes deadly voyages were commonplace, but it took years before legislation could be passed to improve conditions; steamship companies opposed such attempts, fearing it might cut into profits. Not until the 1910s would the shipboard environment improve for third-class passengers.[16]

After I first learned about O. R., I liked to picture him gazing up at the Statue of Liberty, as his ship sailed into the harbor. I was startled to learn that he was not greeted by Liberty, nor did he go through Ellis Island, as they had not yet been built. Most likely, he was processed through Castle Garden, the first official immigrant center. He would be considered "old immigration," a group for the most part composed of western and northern Europeans, and who were primarily Protestant.[17]

There is a record of a twelve-year-old Reinhold Winkler arriving at Castle Garden in New York City from Bremen, Germany, on the ship "Oder" in 1882, the year O. R. left. Reinhold paid for his own ticket, and listed his occupation as farmer, but no other details are recorded. O. R. was, in fact, fourteen at the time, but the information may have been incorrectly recorded or illegible, so perhaps this was my great-grandfather, as cousins descended from Frederick living in Larned and Rozel, Kansas, during the 1930s knew him only as "Reinhold."

Castle Garden began as a harbor fort known as the West Battery in 1807, but was transformed into an immigrant receiving station in 1855 in order to better deal with the immigrants—sometimes a thousand a day during the summer—who were literally dumped onto the waterfront and left to fend for themselves against thieves and predators.[18]

Though Castle Garden's facilities initially helped organize the flood of arrivals, the numbers grew bigger every year, overwhelming the system. Immigrants not processed immediately after arrival had to sleep overnight on benches and floors, while rats and other vermin crawled freely over them.[19] Eastern European Jews began using the term "Kesselgarden" for any confusing, chaotic situation.[20] Federal investigators found that immigrants were charged twice to have their baggage shipped, money-changers did not follow the true market rate, and railroads were making enormous sums from ticket sales.[21]

Finally, the government took control of admitting immigrants away from the states and put it under the jurisdiction of the new Federal Bureau of Immigration. Castle Garden closed in 1890 and Ellis Island began receiving immigrants in 1892. This was the beginning of the New Immigration from eastern and southern Europe; now the new arrivals were mostly Roman Catholic, Jewish, and Eastern Orthodox and the country began to view these poor and non-Protestant immigrants in a different light.[22] Laws were passed to restrict those deemed to be undesirable—Orientals, Jews, anarchists, and labor agitators.

The castle-like fort that processed over eight million immigrants from 1855 to 1890 stayed empty until 1896 when it was turned into an aquarium. Over 5,000 people a day came to see the exotic fish and Beluga whale on display, and it remained a popular attraction until 1941 when it was closed and slated to be demolished. The National Park Service stepped in and restored it so that it looks now much like it did when O. R. came through.[23]

Grandpa told me that Winkler relatives took O. R. in hand in New York and got him on a train to Chicago; no one now remembers who they were. Then from Chicago, it seems likely that he took another train to Lockport, about 35 miles to the southwest. From there he would have to make his own way to where Frederick Winkler had his farm and would take him in. O. R. wandered around the Lockport station, asking passers-by in his broken, German-accented English if they could tell him how to get to the Winkler farm. It didn't take him long to find a German speaker.

It so happened that a farmer named Matthias Wohlgemuth, who had immigrated from Germany in 1854, was hauling a wagonload of lumber, and knew of O. R.'s relatives; indeed, the Winkler's farm adjoined his own property, which was northeast of Lockport about two miles. He offered O. R. a ride and dropped him off. There O. R. had room and board from his uncle and aunt

The Farm on the Wall

and cousins, and helped on their farm.

Eventually O. R.'s siblings followed him across the Atlantic. Anna Lydia, usually known as Lydia, born in 1869, arrived in Lockport in 1887, five years after O.R. She met and married a Mr. Hannes Henry Timm in 1889 in Lockport where their two children were born, but the family ultimately moved to Minnesota, first to Belle Prairie, and then to Little Falls.

I don't know exactly when Frank arrived in Lockport, but it was sometime before 1898, as he appears in the 1st Regiment Illinois Calvary, Co. E of the US Army for that year, in Springfield. It was slated to participate in the Spanish-American War, but never made it out of the country. In September, 1905, he travelled to Little Falls to visit his sister Lydia and her husband. *The Little Falls Herald* noted "Mr. Winkler has been ill for some time, and is here with the hope that the climate will benefit him."[24] He headed to California, where he worked in a lumber mill in Fort Bragg and married one Elizabeth Pohl; they had one daughter that I can trace.

But what about Otto's father? I asked Grandpa. *Did he come over, too?* He did, Grandpa admitted, but he didn't know when, or where he went. Decades later, I found Traugott in the 1900 census for Little Falls, Minnesota, the only evidence I've come across for him. He was 71 years old, and a widower, living with his daughter and son-in-law. *He got homesick*, Grandpa said, *and he went back to Germany. My dad, he told me his father died on board ship, and they buried him out at sea.* O.R. returned to Germany and settled his father's estate. O.R.'s obituary recorded "This was the only time he had left the United States, the country of his choice."[25]

For three years O.R. worked for his uncle, but at 17, he left the farm and went to work in an iron foundry, lured no doubt, by the promise of steady wages. He was an iron and brass molder, Dad told me. Exactly where he first began working, I do not know. The 1896 Lockport City Directory lists him as a brass molder; two years later he is a molder for the Joliet Manufacturing Company. This company, which was in business from 1849 through the

Carol Winkler Kotsch

1930's, produced agricultural implements, primarily corn shellers, plows, and barbed wire. It covered a 10-state region in the Midwest, from Ohio to Nebraska and Kansas.[26]

In the 1900 census, O.R.'s occupation was listed as an iron molder. It was hard, dangerous work, but there were plenty of immigrants around who were willing to do it. From all over Europe they had been coming to Chicago and the surrounding area since the Civil War, attracted to a city that dealt in more grain, cattle, and lumber than anywhere else in the world, thanks to a railroad system that was the hub of ten lines at the time. From a population of 100,000 around 1860, it grew to 300,000 by 1870. When the Great Fire of 1871 burned it down, the city barely paused, and then began to rebuild, this time in skyscrapers of iron and steel. The population jumped to a million by 1890; 79 percent of Chicagoans were born abroad or were children of immigrants.[27]

The great steel mills that made Chicago famous began in the 1850s and were clustered near the Chicago River. The industry grew and spread, supplying iron and steel to build railroads and skyscrapers and bridges in the growing country.[28] Ultimately, it spilled over to the city of Joliet, located about five miles south of Lockport. The Joliet Iron and Steel Works started in 1869 and grew to become the second largest steel mill in the country.[29] Perhaps O.R. was also employed at this company.

Steelworkers endured twelve-hour shifts, with a day off every two weeks, as the blast furnaces had to run continuously. The heat needed to turn raw ore into pig iron was so intense that workers in the hottest areas wore thick-soled shoes, jackets, hats with earflaps, and swathed their faces.[30] Smoked glasses protected eyes from the glare, but little could be done to shield ears from the clamor of the machinery, and many men grew deaf from the noise.[31]

When the white-hot steel was poured, flames shot out, and sometimes the steel slopped over onto unlucky men, causing serious burns.[32] If one of the casks holding the steel fractured, then the mill was flooded with liquid metal and the workers burned alive.[33] As the metal was cast and ground and polished, dust and grit filled the air, irritating the eyes, ears, and throats of the men as they breathed it in. Many suffered from lung diseases years later, especially tuberculosis.[34] Workers began striking in 1910 for better working conditions and shorter hours, but things did not improve until 1923 when at last, under pressure from the public and the president, the industry agreed to an eight-hour-day.[35] It would come too late for O. R.

Despite the shards of metal flying about and the bursts of noxious fumes and scalding steam, O. R. probably felt he was well on his way to realizing the American dream. He had a job, he had become a citizen in 1888—Frederick's son Carl August, better known as Albert, witnessed his naturalization papers—and he was courting a young lady—Mary Wohlgemuth, the daughter of the man who gave him a ride from the train station.

They were married on November 25, 1890, in the Evangelical Church in Lockport, where Mary's parents had been charter members, along with Frederick Winkler and his family. O. R. was 23 years old and Mary 21. In spite of his haphazard early years—or perhaps because of them—he grew to be a committed Christian, recalled my Uncle Lowell; in the fiftieth anniversary souvenir album of the church, published in 1909, O. R. was a member of the board of trustees, along with C.W. Kronmeyer, who also witnessed his naturalization, and his cousin Ed Winkler. He also taught a men's Sunday school class. Mary was the president of the Women's Mission Society.

After their marriage, O. R. and Mary moved into their own home and produced a daughter and three sons: Mae, who was born in 1891; Arthur, whom I knew only as Uncle, in 1893; Irving, my grandfather, in 1895, the same year Montezuma was declared dead by the Kansas legislature; and Lloyd, in 1898.

O. R. became a fervent patriot of his new homeland; Germany was behind him. He never lost his accent, though, and his English was somewhat "ungrammatical," Uncle Lowell remembered—he could be heard singing "bringing in the sheeps" instead of "sheaves" at church—but he continued to write in German to his sister Lydia. Alcohol and playing cards were not allowed in the house.

Their children were surrounded by German-speaking adults, however, and they learned both English and German; Dad thought German was probably his father's first language. Once they started school, English became their primary language, and German was used less and less. I remember that Grandpa taught me to say "danke shoen" for "thank you." When I begged to learn more, he said it was all that he remembered.

Though their father didn't talk much about those early years in Lockport to his children, Dad and Uncle Lowell told me that in the wintertime Grandpa would skate to school when the canal next to their house froze over. This was the Illinois and Michigan Canal, built to connect the Great Lakes and the Mississippi River. Completed in 1848, it carried grain and lumber to Chicago, while sugar, salt, molasses and tobacco were shipped from the southern states.[36] Limestone quarried outside of Lockport went to Chicago and was used to build churches and the Chicago Water Tower.[37] In a few years, the railroads would make the canals obsolete, but they did significantly decrease the cost of shipping, and helped make Chicago the hub of Midwestern trade.[38]

In addition to income from tolls, the Illinois and Michigan also leased 90 feet strip lots along the canal, charging for water power, and for ice leases. But there were also many expenses for the canal, and the horses that pulled the barges. The canal commissioners' report for 1911 showed that disbursements were made for masonry work and lock repair, new windows for offices, rat traps, coal, oil, and boat covers. There were livery expenses for the horses: stable and harness repair, blacksmithing, and veterinary services. For furnishing oats and hay during that year, O.R. received $130.46.[39]

After several years of working in the foundry, O. R.'s lungs were affected by the fumes and the sharp particles of dust that he had breathed. He could no longer keep up with the work and eventually lost his job. In 1905, when my grandpa, Irving, was ten years old, Matthias died. O. R. and Mary moved in with Mary's mother, Margaretta, on the family farm, and the three boys began

The Farm on the Wall

helping with the crops and the dairy herd.

In the fall, O. R. and the boys harvested the corn. As they walked alongside a horse-drawn wagon with a high board on one side, they would grab an ear of corn with one hand, snap it off the stalk with a hook carried in the other hand, and toss it into the wagon where it smacked against the board and tumbled down to land in the ever-growing pile. When the harvest was finished, then the boys would return to school, nearly a month after the rest of the class. My grandpa never quite caught up with the rest of the students, though he was passed along from year to year until he was about thirteen, which was the end of his formal schooling. The 1940 census shows he had an eighth grade education, but it was probably pretty spotty, Uncle Lowell told me.

Every morning, Grandpa helped his mother milk the twelve cows her family owned. His hands would ache from the strain of milking, and he cried as he moved from cow to cow. The fresh milk was poured into ten-gallon cans, thought my dad, and hoisted onto the wagon; milk from the night before, which had been cooling in a water tank overnight, was added. Then there was a hurry to get it from the farm to Lockport where it would be loaded onto the milk train to Joliet.

Arthur, my great-uncle, liked to tell Dad and Uncle Lowell about the time he and brother Irving, my grandpa, raced the neighbor boy to see whose horses would get to the train station first one winter. The horses were wearing shoes with spikes to keep them from slipping on the iced-over roads; the wagon was now fitted with sled runners in place of wheels for winter hauling. Their team was ahead, and Uncle urged them to go a little faster, when for some reason, the horses abruptly balked and stopped. The sled slewed around from behind the horses, leaned over, and the milk cans went tumbling out.

When Mary's mother died in January of 1916, O. R. found himself at a crossroads. The family farm would not go to his wife. Instead, it was sold and the money divided among Mary and her surviving siblings. It was not enough to buy any farmland in Illinois. O.R.'s sons, now grown men, decided to leave. *We'll take*

Carol Winkler Kotsch

our chances out in Kansas, they declared.

O. R. hesitated. His cousins Albert and Fred were already farming out in Pawnee County in western Kansas, but this would be a chancy move, one that would take his family away from the familiar life they had established in Lockport, and out to a dry, sparsely settled part of Kansas that was mostly built on speculation. He decided to go with his sons.

4

Starting from Scratch

Early in March, they put their belongings onto a railroad boxcar—two horses, a couple of cows and a bull, a moldboard plow, a wagon and other farm equipment--and made the journey riding alongside their possessions. When the train stopped to take on water, they seized the chance to unload the horses and cattle and walk them around the train station until it was time to continue the trip. Mary would stay behind in Lockport until a house could be built, but she sent food with them, chiefly canned tomatoes and dried beans.

After unloading at the train depot in Montezuma they rode northwest until they arrived at the surveyor's stakes marking their half-section. It looked different from what he remembered seeing six years ago, O. R. thought, and it was not quite as desirable as he recalled. He wondered if Forrest had shown him one piece of land and sold him another. To his sons, it looked just like every other grass- and cactus-covered section they had passed. *Never mind,* they said; *we'll make it work.*

At first, they slept under the wagon, and hobbled the livestock

Carol Winkler Kotsch

at night and put them on pickets during the day. Until they dug a well, they got water from a Mr. Sweeny, who lived on the quarter section to the south. A building to shelter the livestock and to store grain was the first thing to go up, and then a crude corral. The men partitioned off some rooms in the shed for themselves and set up housekeeping as best they could, with Irving, my grandpa, doing most of the cooking. He would not eat canned tomatoes in later years, though he would slice fresh ones and sprinkle sugar on top, which he taught my brother and me to do.

Now it was critical to get a crop of oats in the freshly plowed sod so the horses could be fed over the winter. The scant buffalo grass would not give them enough energy to plow in the springtime. Somewhere in the collection of old photos belonging to my father is a small picture of a team of horses harnessed to the header that would cut the wheat. They looked thin-sided and rough, not at all like the sleek, well-fed horses I grew up with. A funny-looking shawl that seemed to be made of beads covered their shoulders and sides, which Dad said would brush off the flies as they walked along.

In 1916, *The Annals of Kansas* noted,

> Western Kansas was getting ready to plant wheat. A dispatch from Hutchinson said: "Gas tractors are tearing the whole country upside down in western Kansas, and at the present rate the famous short-grass pasturage will be a thing of the past. Trainloads of tractors have been shipped into that part of the state and are turning the sod and getting the ground ready for cultivation . . . One ranch in Morton county is plowing up 3,000 acres. Another in Ford county [sic] has eleven outfits plowing on the Sherman ranch. Ten tractor outfits were unloaded at Satanta in Haskell county [sic] in two days. Montezuma, in Gray county [sic], received five in one day."[1]

O. R. and his sons were busy plowing their acreage in the spring of that year, but it would be some time before they could afford a gas tractor. Four horses pulled their two-bottom mold-

The Farm on the Wall

board plow, an implement with two plow-shares—triangular blades about a foot wide and 18 to 24 inches long—underneath. The curved moldboard on the edge of the plowshares caught the broken sod and turned it over so that the roots ended up on top. There were wheels on either side of the plow, and a smaller wheel in the back with a steel seat above it where Grandpa or Uncle sat and guided the horses as they turned over the buffalo grass and cactus.

It was a bumpy ride on top of that seat underneath the sun; the horses were always fresh in the morning when they started out, and the driver had to make sure they didn't spend themselves early on. Grandpa and Uncle had wide-brimmed hats for the sun but refused to get an umbrella; it was unnecessary and expensive. Dad didn't drive a tractor with a cab until 1966.

The rattlesnakes that had inhabited the prairie undisturbed for centuries were now being evicted, and the men had to keep watch while working in the field. They were never bit, said Dad, though the horses were struck a couple of times on the legs. There was no vet in the area, but the horses survived and continued to plow, though their legs were painfully swollen for several days. The snakes remained a problem for several years, even after the horses were gone. My grandfather once plowed up a nest of little rattlers, and watched the big ones strike at the steel tractor wheels.

In 1919, a five-year-old boy, playing in his front yard in nearby Copeland, was bitten five times by a rattler. "It was feared he would die from the effects of the poison," *The Montezuma Press* noted, "but this evening reports were to the effect that he was getting better."[2]

The constant plowing and the determined efforts of the area farmers to eradicate them finally did them in, although they lingered here and there. The sand quarter over east and north of the farm couldn't be plowed, but it provided enough pasture to run a few head of cattle. Grandpa and Dad were bumping slowly along in the pickup counting noses when Grandpa brought it to a sudden stop and stared at something in the grass. *You have a shovel in back?* he asked. *I see a rattler.* Dad handed one over, and Grandpa took care of it with a practiced hand. It was a big one—the rattle had seven buttons, which Dad cut off. My brother and I played with it until we wore it out, though I don't remember it.

And once Dad raked one out from under the lilac bush next to the house. I watched from a safe distance as he killed it, eating my strawberry jam sandwich and wondering what all the fuss was about. Bull snakes, however, were left alone to keep the rodents under control, but even spotting one of these was a rare occurrence around the farm and half section as I grew up.

On May 25, 1916, *The Jacksonian* in Cimarron observed, "O.R.Winkler's are working on their new home."[3] The hill that rose on the southeast side of O. R.'s half-section continued on along to Mr. Sweeny's quarter section to the south. He kept pigs on his farm, which he let run loose. O. R. didn't want pigs roaming around the house he planned to build, so he and his sons settled at the bottom of the hill on their section.

The men dug the foundation by hand, tossing each shovelful of soil into their wagon. When it was full, the team pulled the wagon out into the fields, where the dirt was scooped off. To make concrete, they drove the wagon to the sand hills by Wild Horse Lake, about two miles off to the north, and shoveled up what they needed. It wasn't the best quality sand to combine with the cement, but it served for many years, until 1977, when my parents discovered they could not put a new house on top of the foundation, as it was beginning to crumble away.

The lumber for the 900 foot-square house, including the doors and windows, cost $1500. Labor was extra for the carpenter who helped the Winkler men construct the frame and put up the walls and roof. There was no sheetrock then to attach to the bare studs; instead, narrow strips of wood—lathes—were nailed horizontally across the studs with a small gap between each lathe. To finish the wall, plaster was applied from the bottom up and forced through the gaps.

To save some money for the lathe and plaster walls, the Win-

The Farm on the Wall

klers traded work with Benard Koehn and his sons who lived on the north quarter of the section. While working on O. R.'s house, Benard and his sons exchanged remarks about some personal family business. They did not want Arthur and Irving to understand, so they used Plautdietsch, an East Low German dialect taken by the Mennonites to Russia. It was different from the German the Winkler brothers knew, but they understood it well enough. Irving started laughing at something they said. *You understand us?* they said in astonishment. *Ich tue*, he replied. *I do*. After that, they were more careful about what they said in German around the Winkler family.

A well of their own was next. Once again, The *Jacksonian* recorded on June 18, 1916, "O.R. Winkler decided it was nice to have a windmill, and an engine, too, so he took out a new mill the other day." They hired a well driller, who went down about 120 feet to reach water. This first windmill was a wooden tower with wooden blades. When O. R. and Mary moved to Montezuma in 1922, the town did not yet have a water system, and all the homes had windmills in the backyard. Sometime after O. R. died in 1941, and a modern water system was installed, the windmill in his backyard was moved out to the farm to replace the wooden tower. One day in the mid-sixties, it stopped bringing up water. The well driller re-drilled, going down this time to 200 feet. I watched as he pulled a long tree root out of the old pipe, where it had been seeking easy water.

There was an outhouse located about 30 feet of the northwest corner of the house, but it had been moved by the time the picture was taken in '55. And yes, your grandfather and his family used the pages from the Montgomery Ward and Sears catalogs. After Grandpa installed the butane gas tank in '38, they also added a hot water heater so that Grandma no longer had to heat water on the coal stove. Now there was hot and cold running water and they finished out a bathroom with a tub and a toilet and began buying toilet paper to use. Grandma wanted the outhouse moved out of sight, and it was hauled over to the south side of the long shed. It's hard to see in the picture.

Carol Winkler Kotsch

The outhouse stayed there all the time I was growing up, and I can recall having to use it myself once or twice when the power was out, but otherwise it was largely abandoned, and the wasps found it an ideal place to build nests. Sometimes the chickens would lay eggs on the floor and I would reach in very cautiously to get them. Eventually Dad moved it over to the Schmidt property east of the farm.

The basement walls and ledges remained made of dirt until the early 1940s when there was a little extra money, and Grandma decreed that it would be spent on improving the basement. This time Grandpa hauled the sand from Dodge City in a pickup. Dad and Uncle Lowell mixed the sand and cement together, and then they stacked concrete blocks around the walls, plastered them, and poured a layer of concrete on top of the ledges. When they finished, they signed their names and the date in the wet concrete. It was covered with spider webs and dust when I found their signatures many years later, but I could still read "Lowell and Riley Winkler, 1942."

On June 29, 1916, *The Montezuma Press* noted that "O.R. Winkler northwest of town, has completed a fine new barn, and has a nice two-story house enclosed." The old farmhouse did indeed have a tall roof, and full attic that Dad remembered you could stand upright in without bumping your head, but it was never turned into a living space. With the house and windmill finished, Mary made the trip from Lockport to join them, and they posed for a picture on the south-facing porch. The men are dressed identically in suits and jackets and ties, with old-fashioned high collars on their shirts, and wearing flat working man's caps; Mary is wearing long skirts and a white blouse.

There were a few sod houses—soddies—around, but they were the exception rather than the rule. Though cheap and relatively easy to build, they were damp on the inside, and were infested with insects and mice, which attracted snakes. If it rained, the roof might collapse, and when it was dry, the dirt would crumble away. Samuel Gordon and his wife raised their four daughters in one about a mile and a half west of our farm, Dad remembered.

The Farm on the Wall

They eventually built a wooden frame around the sod, which provided excellent insulation, but it was so close and cramped on the inside, Dad recalled seeing a haze when he stopped by to help the family, and the kerosene lamp wouldn't burn for lack of oxygen.

Like many settlers to the high plains, O. R. and his sons were quick to plant trees around their home for shade and a windbreak, turning each farmstead into a small island in the sea of buffalo grass. But to my mother's exasperation years later, O. R. planted trees only on the east and west sides of the house. The rough-looking elms on the east and the more stately maples on the west did indeed provide some shade, but there was nothing to shield the house from the constant south winds which whistled through the cracks in the winter; sometimes I would find a thin layer of snow on my windowsill.

In time, the branches all leaned toward the north. The northern-most tree in the row of elms on the east side of the house, the one closest to the water supply, was also the biggest; the rest of the trees diminished in size, like nesting dolls, as they were out of reach of the water hose and had to rely on rainfall to survive. The very last and smallest tree bent the most from receiving the full blast of the south winds.

The big maple tree on the west side of the house was the best one for climbing; its trunk divided low to the ground, making it easy to scramble up. Sometimes I would inch out along a nearly horizontal branch and make it sway up and down before I crept back. It produced thousands of winged seeds in the spring, and I tossed them into the air and watched them spin to the ground like helicopter blades. In the fall I raked up the leaves and burned them in the trash can and roasted hot dogs and marshmallows on a thin branch I broke off.

There were a couple of mulberry trees around the farm, but not close to the house, as the soft fruit stained badly and made a mess on the ground. They were harder to climb, but I persisted in order to reach the mulberries. Sometimes I would declare to my mother that I was going to pick enough so she could make a pie, but I always ate them before I brought the bowl back to the house.

Carol Winkler Kotsch

    The move from Lockport, and the new house had used up much of O. R.'s savings, and his sons took turns hiring themselves out to area farmers, or even traveling to other towns for work, while the others stayed behind and helped O. R. with his crops. On July 1, 1917, *The Jacksonian* noticed that "Arthur and Lloyd Winkler have gone east to harvest."[4] Irving, my grandfather, traveled to Stafford that fall and shucked corn for a dollar a day. His face froze from the cold, but the money he brought back kept them going.

    Ultimately, Lloyd, the youngest brother, decided that farming was not for him. He headed west to Colorado and worked in the steel mill in Pueblo, but it was just as back-breaking as farming and he only stayed for two years. Looking for something less strenuous, he moved back to Chicago and studied to be a chiropractor, but that, too, did not work. He applied for the Chicago police force, but since he was wearing glasses, he was turned down. The Detroit police force, however, did not place any restrictions on glasses and he was accepted. He stayed in Detroit for the rest of his life and started his family there. Sister Mae remained in Chicago; she found work as a secretary, eventually married James Taggart and moved to California, and never lived on the farm in Kansas.

5

The Great War, the Flu, and a Dare

After just a couple of years of plowing, planting, and building, their efforts to develop the farm were interrupted. It was a war—the Great War—that slowed them down temporarily and brought my grandparents together. All three of the Winkler brothers registered for the draft—Irving and Arthur in June 1917, and Lloyd in September of 1918—but it was Irving, my grandpa, who was called up. His draft registration card shows him to have been of medium height and build, with blue eyes and light brown hair. Irving further declared that he was needed at home.

He enlisted at the Cimarron Courthouse on July 14, 1918, when he was almost 23 years old. He was first shipped to Camp Funston at Fort Riley, a training camp created shortly after war was declared in April 1917. Covering some 2,000 acres, it was a temporary home to over 50,000 men, most of them from Kansas and other Plains states.[1]

The pacifist German-Russian Mennonites in Gray County, and all across Kansas, however, objected to the war and refused to enlist. Some were imprisoned in military facilities where they were harshly treated and physically abused for being conscientious objectors. Eventually, because of a shortage of farm labor, many were released for farm service or relief work overseas.

In Montezuma, they refused to contribute to the Liberty Loan, liberty bonds sold during war that helped cover the war expenses of the United States. For over a year they had been pressured to contribute by a local committee, but they responded in a letter to *The Press* in the spring of 1918 that "disobedience to the command of Christ means everlasting death." They also pointed out that they had "organized a relief committee for the hungry and starving in war stricking country [sic] for which we hold collections once a month in all our congregations. . . ."[2]

With that response, they became targets across the county. Any Mennonite man who refused to buy a bond was dry-shaved, Dad said, but *The Press* mentioned that barber's clippers were used; Bernhard H. Koehn was the first Mennonite to lose his beard.[3] A few others refused and were shaved, but most gave in and bought a bond. After another conference, this time in Wichita with the chairman of the state loan on hand, Mennonites offered to donate money to the government without having to take Liberty bonds, even offering to sell their wheat at pre-war "peace" prices.

The chairman, Charles L. Davidson, was impressed by their earnestness to avoid any contributions that would aid the fighting, and eventually, a compromise was reached that Mennonites would buy their full quota of bonds, but that the bonds would be given to the Red Cross and the Y.M.C.A.[4]

Anti-German feeling ran high all across the United States, and many German families were persecuted and harassed. German-American schools closed and German newspapers ceased publication, German books were burned, and citizens with German names were pressured into anglicizing them, or changed them out of fear of retaliation. Even streets with German names were changed. In Kansas, German classes were abolished in the Dodge City High School, and Spanish was substituted for German at Ellsworth.[5] The German-American Alliance of Kansas met at Leavenworth in 1916 and declared their allegiance to the United

The Farm on the Wall

States.⁶ Despite their German background, O. R. and his family were not molested. It helped, of course, that his son was in the service, but O. R. was a faithful American citizen and devoted to his adopted country.

With Irving gone, his share of the work fell to Arthur and Lloyd. The demand for wheat grew as the war disrupted farmers in Europe. Russia, the main supplier, was cut off, which opened up the market to the United States. "Food will win the war," declared propaganda posters, and Americans were encouraged to observe wheatless Mondays so soldiers would be well fed. The price for a bushel of wheat rose to a dizzying high of $2 in 1917, prices that wouldn't return until the Fifties.⁷

Tempted by these high prices, farmers plowed under still more grass, and more sheep and cattle were crowded onto fewer acres of grazing land, which was churned under sharp hooves and eaten down to the roots. The sea of grass that covered the plains quickly disappeared. The rains kept coming, however, and the dust settled and the grass that was left grew again, and the golden fields of wheat went on for mile after mile. It was like the gold rush of the 1840s, except the gold now grew from the soil.

It was the beginning of another boom and bust cycle that would bedevil farmers again over the decades. I saw something very similar in 1972 when poor harvests in Russia triggered wheat sales. Prices began to go up from a monthly average of $1.33 in June 1972 to $2.43 a year later. Then in August, 1973, it jumped to a monthly average of $4.45. We watched the market report constantly, and little else was talked about over coffee at the drugstore. Would it make it to $5? Farmers began plowing land that had been taken out of production, land that should have been left untilled, Dad said. Six months later, in February, 1974, it was $5.52. It was hard to resist such easy profits, and many farmers bought big-ticket items on credit. And then, the inevitable happened—the average dropped to $3.57 that June, and went up and down after that, mostly down.

The boom created by the war was good news for the fledgling Winkler farm, and while his ruined lungs could not take the stress of hard work, O. R. did what he could to help. One morning, though, while harnessing the horses, one of them restlessly tossed its head and struck O. R. in the face, sending his glasses flying, and giving him a black eye. *The Montezuma Press* reported in September of 1918 that he was recovering nicely, though he still could not find his glasses, and that Mrs. Winkler was now harnessing the horses.[8]

Like all new arrivals to Camp Funston, Irving took a cold shower, and was then inspected for communicable diseases; measles, German measles, mumps, meningitis, and tuberculosis were easily spread in the close quarters.[9] The men received required inoculations—Grandpa's enlistment record notes he was inoculated for typhoid and paratyphoid on August 3—and was quarantined for three weeks. None of this would be of any help for something much worse—the Spanish flu.

Several locations and dates have been put forth as the origin of the flu—New York, China, and France, from soldiers who served in Indochina—but such a large pandemic makes it hard to determine exactly where and when.[10] However, there was an outbreak not 20 miles from the Winkler farm. In late January and early February of 1918 in Haskell County, the local physician, Dr. Loring Miner, began treating cases of the flu. Just a couple at first, and then more and more, until he counted 18 patients stricken with severe influenza. He became the first to report the unusual cases to the U.S. Public Health Service, but nothing was done.[11]

In Haskell County, *The Santa Fe Monitor* noted

> Mrs. Eva Van Alstine is sick with pneumonia. Ralph Lindeman is still quite sick. Homer Moody has been reported quite sick. Mertin, the young son of Ernest Elliot, is sick with pneumonia. Ralph McConnell has been quite sick this week. Most everybody over the county is having lagrippe or pneumonia.[12]

Local boys home on leave from Fort Riley arrived in the midst of an illness that no one understood. Ernest, father of the sick

Mertin, went to Funston to visit his brother.[13] On March 11, a soldier reported sick with a bad cold, the first case of what would become known as "Spanish flu."[14] At the end of the day 100 soldiers reported sick and over half died from the fluid that filled their lungs. Within three weeks, 1,100 soldiers had symptoms of the flu.[15] The ones who recovered were shipped out overseas and from there the flu and the subsequent pneumonia spread across Europe, hitting Spain especially hard, and then world-wide, eventually killing 20-50 million people by some estimates.

Irving contracted the flu shortly after he arrived; his case may have been the milder version of the first wave, before it mutated into a more lethal version. Still, he began running a high fever, typical of its symptoms. Doctors of the day knew nothing of the viruses that caused influenza, and they developed mostly useless vaccines to kill what was thought to be a bacterial infection. When modern science failed, people turned to folk remedies, immersing themselves in strong-smelling substances like turpentine and camphor, or inhaling sulfur heated over coals, in the belief that the powerful odor would drive out the disease. In Grandpa's case, he was given ice-water baths in a canvas bathtub to bring down the fever, and he slowly recovered.

The flu continued for the rest of the summer, into the fall of 1918. On October 8, 1400 soldiers were stricken within twenty-four hours at Camp Funston, and then it simply stopped.[16] Officials declared the worst was over.

In Montezuma, however, the schools closed in October 1918 and didn't reopen until December 30. *The Montezuma Press* noted "the influenza outbreak seems to be pretty well stamped out, and we have no fears of another outbreak, though of course, there is always that possibility to guard against."[17] But just two months later in late March several students and teachers were still absent due to the flu.[18] In January, 1920, 700 new cases of flu were reported across Kansas.[19]

Grandpa was first trained as a carpenter at Camp Funston, and helped construct some of the buildings, Uncle Lowell remembered his father telling him, though most of the camp had been already been completed by December 1917. He was housed with 200 other men in one of the many barracks in the camp. Each boasted electric lights, steam heat, and hot and cold running water.[20] It was probably the first time he had ever experienced such modern conveniences, my dad thought.

He also learned to play pool while at Camp Funston, as the soldiers needed some form of recreation. The "Zone of Department of Camp Activities and Amusements" included three theaters, a pool hall with 70 tables, bowling alleys, barbershops, three Knights of Columbus Halls, and 14 YMCA buildings, not to mention restaurants and "stores with complete lines of merchandise."[21] Grandpa got to be a pretty good shot with a pool stick, Dad recalled, but he couldn't play when he returned home, as most pool tables were in beer halls, and that was something his mother would not permit.

Grandpa would do more than learn carpentry, however; Camp Funston was also used as basic training for balloon companies. When that was finished, he was sent to the recently completed Fort John Wise in San Antonio, Texas, late in September, 1918, when he became part of 3rd Co. 164th Depot Brigade Balloon Battalion, the 79th Balloon Company. When the flu hit Fort Wise, the balloon companies were quarantined and scattered to complete their training. The 79th was sent to nearby Camp Travis.[22]

The mission of the 102 balloon companies formed during what proved to be the final months of the war, was to report overseas to the front, and launch a balloon to report on the enemy's movements. [23] *The Stars and Stripes* reported in France in 1918 that

> A sausage is an observation balloon, anchored to a motor truck by piano wire. The truck is to move the wire out of range when enemy guns take long range shots at the sau sage. The balloon follows the wire.
>
> The observer is the occupant of the sausage basket. His job...is to report to his friends on the ground by tele-

The Farm on the Wall

phone—especially as to the effects of artillery fire from his own side...if an enemy avion [sic] comes very close and be gins shooting incendiary bullets through the sausage, the observer is supposed to leap out into the empty air. Down he plunges for 300, 400 or 500 feet then...the large light white parachutes attached to his back will float out..."[24]

The 250 men in each company went through a usual camp routine: daily drill, kitchen duty, and washing their uniforms. Then they broke up for more specialized training, learning to repair the fabric of the balloons, hydrogen generation and storage, balloon rigging, basket repair, parachute rigging, and balloon handling.[25]

For Irving, it also meant learning how to handle and fire a machine gun on the firing range. If the enemy advanced while the balloon was spying out troop movements, his job would be to defend the pilot and crew of the balloon, as well as the men who raised and lowered it on the winch truck.

Another soldier from Kansas was serving in the same company, Ernest Graves, from the northeastern town of Troy in Doniphan County. You can see them both in the panoramic picture of the balloon company that Grandpa brought back. The large picture, a foot wide and over three feet long, was probably a "kidnapped" photograph, so dubbed by studio photographers because the pictures were taken with no financial obligation to the subject, and then offered for sale.[26] I had only known my grandfather as an old man, of course, so it was hard at first for me to recognize the young soldier wearing what looked like a forest ranger's hat—the men referred to them as "sombreros"[27]—and laced-up leggings to protect his shins.

Ernest struck up a friendship with my grandfather and decided that Irving was a suitable young man to view a picture of his sisters, unlike the other soldiers who ran around San Antonio while off duty, gawking at the big city sights, drinking, and chasing girls. In that day and time, Ernest, as the older brother, was responsible for looking after his sisters, Nellie, Lura, and Ruth, who could not see any men without his approval. When the sisters learned about their brother's new acquaintance, Nellie dared Lura to write to a soldier, and so she did, feeling rather bold.

After the balloon company's training was completed, the men were put on a train to be shipped overseas. While the train was somewhere in Georgia, according to Uncle Lowell, the Armistice was signed, and Irving never left the United States. He was honorably discharged from the army on March 21, 1919, from Camp Funston. Pocketing his pay of $129.05, plus a $50 bonus, he took a train—at a reduced rate for his service—back to Cimarron. *The Press* marked his return a couple of weeks later: "Irving Winkler and Clarence Potts are two more of the Montezuma boys who have arrived home after serving in the army."[28]

Irving had only been home a short time when his chronic appendicitis flared up; it was worse than ever, and the local doctor said the appendix had to come out. There was no surgeon in Dodge City; the only option was to go the hospital in Halstead, founded in 1902 by Arthur Hertzler, the "Horse and Buggy Doctor," and well-known for the quality of its medical care at a time when good doctors were far and few between, let alone a hospital.

Halstead, though, was about 180 miles from the farm, too far for the horse and wagon. Instead, Arthur drove him to Montezuma, bumping for several miles over the rough roads, where Irving took the train to Dodge City, a freight train that also hauled coal. He made himself as comfortable as he could in the caboose, where there was at least a cot where he could lie down, and then switched trains at Dodge, riding the rest of the way to Halstead on a passenger train. The appendix was removed uneventfully, and Irving made a complete recovery after a few days in the hospital. The bill for the surgery and hospital stay was $50; it took a year to pay it off.

After his recovery, Irving joined the American Legion, created by a group of 20 American officers at the behest of Theodore Roosevelt as the war ended; it was intended to serve as a veterans' organization, a support group and a social club to help newly-returned servicemen adjust to civilian life. Most small towns like Montezuma had a Legion Hall somewhere on Main Street. Ours became a multi-purpose building; movie hall, church—my senior prom was held there. He kept his membership cards tucked away, faithfully turning in his dues every year, even during the Depression. He paid $3 in 1944.

Grandpa brought the picture of his balloon company back with him—it was probably rolled up into a tube, Dad thought—but it was never displayed in the house; instead, it stayed curled up in a box of family photos for decades until my father had it carefully unrolled and framed. It must have been a bit of a splurge for my grandfather to purchase that photograph, but his brief time of service—not even a year—surely made an impression on a young man who had spent most of his life in a small town and an isolated farm. He'd seen a bit of the world, said Dad, and Uncle was a bit jealous of his brother's experiences.

The uniform was also stored away, but I can remember seeing it when my brother and I played in the basement of my grandparents' Dodge City home. I wanted to investigate it further, but my fussy aunt shooed me away. After Grandpa died and she inherited the house, she tossed it away without so much as a by-your-leave.

6

To Kansas from the South

Irving continued to write to Lura. He was not an eloquent, well-educated man, and was better with numbers than words, but something in his letters spoke to her. In late January of 1921, he travelled over 350 miles by train to visit Ernest in Troy, but it was really Lura he went to meet. Ironically, she was in the hospital in St. Joseph having her appendix removed. "She is swiftly recovering from the operation at this writing," noted *The Kansas Chief*.[1]

The Graves family was more sophisticated and refined than the Johnny-come-lately Winklers, but they belonged to the genteel poor. David Graves, Lura's father, raised cattle, and grew corn and watermelons, but Grandpa later told Dad their property wasn't very good for farming. Though glaciers had left deposits of fertile loess soil up to thirty feet deep in Doniphan County, David's fields were hilly, and full of draws that could not be plowed. Farmers in other parts of the world lined mountains and hills with raised banks like steps to hold back the water, but terrace farming was unknown or ignored in Kansas at that time; the Graves property literally washed away with each storm. Not until the 1940s would the land round Troy be terraced and the soil saved.

On her father's side, she was descended from Jacob Graves, son of a German immigrant, who appears to have been forced to fight with the British during the Revolutionary War.[1] From the original home in Berks County, Pennsylvania, the Graves family went south to North Carolina, west to Tennessee, and then to Missouri, always seeking better land, before they ended up in Kansas.

Around 1796, Jacob's son John moved to Sharp's Chapel, Union County, in eastern Tennessee. He married his cousin, Sarah Sharp, and their 10 children were born there. Uncle Lowell gave me a piece of fabric that was supposed to come from the curtains in the family plantation, but he didn't know where it was or precisely who owned it. More than likely, the "plantation" was a large farm, as eastern Tennessee was mountainous and not suited for the cotton plantations found in the western part of the state and other areas of the South.[2]

Because of this, slaves were found mostly inside the house as servants instead of field hands, a mark of status and luxury for their owner.[3] They made up only 8 percent of the population in eastern Tennessee as opposed to 40 percent in the west portion of the state.[4] John's household listed two slaves in the 1840 census, a girl under 10 years of age, and a female, possibly her mother, who was between the ages of 36 and 54. His mother would have been horrified to find out that her family once owned slaves, Uncle Lowell said; he was sure she did not know.

The area had also been settled by Quakers from Pennsylvania who arrived at about the same time as John Graves. The Friends, who abhorred slavery, formed the Manumission Society of Tennessee in 1814, and east Tennessee became the home of the first abolitionist movement.[5] The anti-slavery sentiment led to the organization of some 25 manumission societies before 1830.[6]

John and most of his children seemed to be established in Tennessee, but in 1842, his sons Solomon and Anthony left for Missouri, along with their families. The U.S. government had bought

The Farm on the Wall

some two million acres of virgin land—the Platte Purchase—from the Ioway, Sac and Fox Indians in 1836 for $7500.[7] Families from tired-out farms in Illinois, Kentucky, Louisiana, Tennessee, and Virginia poured in to lay claim to the fertile, loess soil of northwestern Missouri, which became the counties of Andrew, Atchison, Buchanan, Holt, Nodaway, and Platte.

John gave his two slaves to Anthony, his second son, who sold them for eleven hundred dollars in silver in order to transport his family to DeKalb in Buchanan County.[8] Perhaps Solomon, the oldest, received a cash settlement for the journey. They began farming in the area, but as soon as the Kansas-Nebraska Bill was passed twelve years later in 1854, Solomon's three sons, Daniel, Isaac, and Sampson immediately left Missouri for Kansas, and settled in Doniphan County, just across the Missouri River. Solomon remained behind in DeKalb.

I do not know why they left. Perhaps the grass simply looked greener, and they were tempted by fertile land in Kansas. Or it may be that they had developed anti-slavery attitudes and found it hard to stay in Missouri where tension was increasing over slavery and state's rights. Southern settlers found that hemp, used for making rope, and tobacco grew very well in the river bottoms in the Platte Purchase area. Cultivating and processing hemp was hard work, however, and required slave labor to make money.[9] Whatever the reason, they and several other families settled first at Mosquito Creek, a small stream north of the city of Troy, but later sold their claims and moved elsewhere in the region. Isaac, Lura's grandfather, purchased 190 acres of land about one and a half miles north of Troy.[10]

In 1859, just a few years after the Graves brothers and their families settled in Doniphan County, Abraham Lincoln was considering running for the presidency. He had been invited to "Bleeding Kansas" by an old legal colleague, Mark Delahay, to speak against slavery, and this seemed like a good opportunity to polish his speech and see how it was received. He came first to Elwood, Kansas, on November 30, and delivered his Kansas speech condemning slavery at the Great Western Hotel. Among the listeners was a delegation of prominent citizens from Troy who were interested in having Lincoln speak in their town as well: Judge J. B. Maynard, Henry Boder, Joe Hayton, and one John Frank Kotsch, who would become your father's great-grandfather.[11]

John Kotsch was born in 1834 in Hamberglin, Bavaria, Germany. He immigrated to the United States in 1852, when he was 16 years old, a stowaway, according to family stories. Your Aunt Kate said that his father was a university professor who spoke seven languages. I haven't been able to verify it, but it seems very likely, with this background, that perhaps the Kotsch family became involved in the German revolutions of 1848. Many of the "Forty-Eighters," as they were called, "favored unification, constitutional government, and guarantees of human rights,"[12] and fought in the Civil War for the Union.

When the revolution failed, they had to leave in a hurry. John went first to Cincinnati, and stayed with a sister, Anna, and learned the shoe-making trade. He moved to Doniphan County in 1857, began making boots and shoes, and established himself within the community.

When Lincoln finished speaking at Elwood, Maynard and the rest of the delegates persuaded him to travel to Troy the next day. The weather was reported to be bitterly cold; Lincoln went by open buggy, wrapped in a buffalo robe for the 12-13 mile trip.[13] He delivered his two-hour speech in the Doniphan County courthouse; when he was finished, a former Kentuckian, and now the largest slaveholder in Kansas was called on to reply.[14] Lincoln spoke two more times in Kansas—at Atchison and Leavenworth—before heading back to Illinois. The speeches were successful, but did not increase his popularity in Kansas; the Kansas delegation did not support him in the Republican convention of 1860.[15]

In the spring of 1861, the tensions between slavery and anti-slavery states finally boiled over. The Kansas State Militia began forming regiments, and on September 27, 1861, John Kotsch was mustered in as a private at Elwood, Kansas. Isaac Graves, and his brothers Daniel and Sampson, also enlisted as privates. Their tour of duty was short-lived, as they were relieved less than a month later. Isaac and Daniel remained privates in the Kansas State Militia, serving intermittently during the Civil War, and finally participating in the battle to repel Price's Raid on the Kansas-Missouri border in October 1864—the Battle of Mine Creek, the largest cavalry engagement during the Civil War.

After another short stint in the militia, this time as a third lieutenant from November, 1861, to January 1862, John went on to enlist in the 13th Kansas Regiment, Company B on September 1, 1862. He was mustered at Atchison, "and wishing to leave his property to his sweetheart in case he did not return," he took her—Mary Ann Newman, daughter of English immigrants—to St. Benedict's Catholic Church in Atchison where they were married on October 2. Their names were Latinized on the register: John Franciscus Kotsch and Maria Anna Newman. He then joined his regiment, and Mary Ann lived with her parents while he was gone.

John Kotsch was one of four first sergeants in the regiment; among the 12 corporals was Sampson Graves, brother of Isaac. While the 13th was fighting in Arkansas, at the Battle of Prairie Grove, a Minié ball passed through John's upper lip and tore out the roof of his mouth, resulting in the loss of six teeth and a cut tongue. Dr. Joseph Whelen, who testified in John's petition for a pension in 1873, noted that flattened bullet "lodged in the root of the tongue, considerable [sic] injuring permanently his articulation."

Because of his conduct during the battle, he was promoted to first lieutenant on May 27, 1863, but his wound continued to trouble him, and a march through the Cherokee Nation seems to have resulted in sunstroke. He was finally discharged in May 1864. He returned to Troy and Mary Ann and became well-known for manufacturing boots and shoes, and for his grapes. He remembered ever after his meeting with Lincoln in 1859, how he sat at the same table with him at the hotel in Troy where Lincoln was a guest, and how Lincoln asked him two times to pass the gingerbread.[16]

Another witness, though, remembered that incident differently. Zenus Smith, the teenage son of the owner of the hotel where Lincoln stayed when he arrived in Troy, claimed that Lincoln

Carol Winkler Kotsch

"asked for and ate several helpings of 'Johnny cakes.'"[17]

Isaac Graves also returned to Troy, where he continued farming, and helped found the Baptist church. He, too, was among the 40 or so listeners at Lincoln's speech at the Troy County Courthouse, which he never forgot. Lura, his granddaughter, listened to stories about Isaac and Lincoln's appearance in Troy, and passed that along to Dad.

On her mother's side, Lura was descended from the Etherton family. Her maternal grandfather, James Alexander Etherton, also came from east Tennessee—Cocke County, which was southeast of Union County where the Graves family lived, and bordered North Carolina. The town of Parrottsville, where he was born, was named for his mother's grandfather, John Parrott, a Revolutionary War soldier whose father Frederick had immigrated from Switzerland or Alsace-Lorraine around 1737.[18]

John was born in 1740 in the Shenandoah Valley of Virginia where his parents had moved from Pennsylvania. John and his six brothers all fought in the Revolutionary War, with John enlisting at the rather advanced age of 37, leaving behind a wife and family. It may have been the needs of his family that led him to desert in 1779 after serving only 14 months of his three-year commitment, during which he was often reported sick or in the hospital in a company that had been decimated by smallpox. He remarried just 22 months later, so his desertion may have been due to the illness or death of his first wife, Catharina Miar or Meyer.[19]

After the war, new land was open for settlement, and though John owned considerable acreage in the Shenandoah Valley, the opportunity to be a new settler in a thinly populated wilderness was tempting. He moved his family to Green County, Tennessee in 1787, where they settled near Clear Creek, and this settlement became known as Parrottsville. His sons George and Jacob, ran a popular tavern on the Old Stage Road.[20] Green County was later reorganized and renamed as Cocke County in 1797 after Senator William Cocke.

About the Etherton family I know very little, only that James's father was George B., who was a farmer in Cocke County and is listed as being an early settler to the area. The name is English, and is a common one in census records for eastern Tennessee. George married Julia Parrott around 1840. James, the second child, was born in 1845.

Whatever kind of farm George had is lost now, but his son James recorded that he took corn to the mill to be ground and fed to the horses; farmers in the fertile river bottoms in Cocke County also produced tobacco and cotton. Wheat and corn and oats were grown, and then ground in the grist mills found by almost every stream. The rivers also provided power for saw mills and woolen mills and carding mills. It was also good country for growing apples, and Cocke County would produce more than any other county in Tennessee.[21] Altogether, it was proving to be a prosperous and growing area, and looked to remain that way.

After Lincoln was elected in November 1860, South Carolina seceded that December, and was followed by nine other states. Tennessee, however, resisted. The first referendum in 1861 had a majority vote against secession, with East Tennessee rejecting it overwhelmingly, and West Tennessee supporting it and Middle Tennessee going both ways. Secession talk would not go away, and a second vote ended up in favor of leaving the Union. At that point, East Tennessee counties petitioned the legislature to leave the rest of the state, but in reply, the state sent an army to oversee the "traitors."[22]

When he was an old man, James sat down and wrote an account of what life was like in Parrotsville just as the war started. He was 16 years old and noticed that "The Excitement was So great there were Severl old men went out & Hung them Selves," and added that a suicide's ghost could still be seen each evening riding his white mule where he had hanged himself, but "I never Seen him my Self So I will Just Write what I have hiard others Say: &You can believe or not."

Once the Confederates had control of the eastern region, pro-Unionists had to remain quiet. James and his family were secret abolitionists, smuggling food to Union sympathizers hiding

Carol Winkler Kotsch

in the nearby woods, who were unable to leave the area.

> ...there was many of our neighbors that were union men and would not go in the Rebil army they was staying out in the Woods near the mountain. Some of them come home to get Some Provisions & Mr. Hale & myself was helping them Carry there Load of grul as we then called it.

James and Mr. Hale were caught by Rebel soldiers as they were leaving. He thought they would be left alone, but

> ...they haulted us and wanted to know where we had been we told them we had only been up the rod a little wayes they begin to Curse us & Say they Knowed we had been out to feed Some of them Toryes & Said they were going to Shoot us and begin to form a circle round us; I begin to think our time was abought up & While they were Cursing & abusing us a thought come to my mind that was the Cause of us not being Shot my Grand Father Lived neare to where we had gon & he had & exclent Possum doge: & I Said to the Rebil Boyes that were standing with there guns Pointed at us. You are mistaken about us being out Feeding the Toreys we went up to Grandfathers to go Hunting & the old Fool Doge would not follow us & we are on our way home I Told this in Such hard Earnis they thought I was telling them the truth.

He also described a skirmish between Union soldiers led by Jim Lane who challenged the Rebel leader Captain Gorman to battle in 1862, and ambushed them about six miles outside of Parrotsville. This was not James H. Lane, the controversial Union general and Kansas senator who fought in Kansas and Missouri, but possibly one of several Tennessee soldiers named Jim Lane fighting for the Union.

> ...the capton tells us all to take a good vew of his Breave men: they were going to Lick old Jim & his cowardly men

The Farm on the Wall

So bad they will never want any one to See them any more. All is read: the command is given Forward March & the crowd gives them three Cheers I heard Some of the croud Say they felt Sorry for Lane & his men for they would all be killed they thought that company of men strung out marching a Longe was able to charge & Capture any amoun of men I can almost See these men yet they are almost to where the Batle is to be faught they are still in high Spirits naw liston they are Entering the Reveane where Lane & his men are cosealed be hind the Large Trees Lane is to fire the first shot & then his men are to fire Lane Steps from be hind a Tree & takes Gormans horse bi the Bridal Shoots Gorman through the body. Lanes men all fired & Gorman men was so excited they forgot to Shoot horses & men tumbled & fell over one another Lane & his men wounded & Captured Gorman and Severil of his men those that was Lucky anuff to get away never stoped Runing there Horses till they got back to Parrottsville a distance of Six Miles they didant come back in such fine stile as they went out for they were scattered all along the Road.

James also witnessed a lynching of a Union prisoner:

...they Took him north of The Town on a high ridge & hung him to a lim of a large White Oak tree they Left him hanging all that day & night & till noon the next day when they Sent his Wife Word for to come & get him that Eavning or they would Feed his body to the Hoges.

James hung around their camp "nearly Every day learning all I could that would be of any beafit to the union boys they thought I was all right I would tell them I was goin into the Army as Soon as I was old anuff but I didant Say what Army I was going into."

Men from the eastern counties who could get out fled to other states in order to enlist for the Union. "Ultimately, some 31,000

Carol Winkler Kotsch

Tennesseans joined the Federal forces, more soldiers than all the other Confederate states together provided to the Union side."[23] James and his older brother Charles both joined the Eighth Tennessee Infantry, K Company in 1863, and marched with Sherman to Atlanta. Charles was killed in April 1864, and James was severely wounded in the thigh just a few months later in August at the Battle of Utoy. He recovered, but his injury troubled him for the rest of his life and made it hard for him to farm.

Grammie told me that after his discharge, he returned to his hometown of Parrotsville, but some of the neighbors still faithful to the lost Confederate cause resented his disloyalty, and headed to his parent's house. Somehow, his mother got word of their plans, Grammie said, and hid James under a feather mattress when they pushed their way in the door. The neighbors overlooked him and left. It must have been hard to show his face as he recovered from his wound, but he remained in Parrotsville until about 1867, when he headed west to DeKalb, Missouri. He married Lucinda Roberts, and they lived there for 12 years, farming and raising a family before they uprooted and moved to another farm in Troy, where he raised wheat and apples.

Their daughter, Arria, was born in 1871 in DeKalb, and moved with her parents to Troy. There she met and married Isaac's son, David, in 1892. They had five children: Ernest, who served with my grandfather Irving during World War I, was born in 1893; Nellie, in 1895—she would become my great-aunt when she married Irving's brother, Arthur; Lura, my grandmother, in 1896, William, in 1900, and Ruth, the baby of the family, in 1904.

With just a year between them, Lura and Nellie were very close as sisters; William was the only sibling I remember Grammie telling me about. He liked to draw, and when he was 12 years old, he sketched a picture of children in a sleigh drawn by a single horse, and titled it, "On their way to Grandmother's for Thanksgiving." *The Kansas Chief* declared that it was "very creditable for of a boy of his age." The editor would like to have printed it in the paper, but *The Chief* "would have to send it away to have a plate made from it and that would take too long. It is also quite expensive to make plates to print from."[24] Just a few weeks later, William won a prize of one dollar in a Christmas contest sponsored by the paper. This time he had drawn "Old Santa with his sled and reindeer driving across country on his Christmas visits."[25]

William's name shows up from time to time in *The Chief*, mostly in connection with family events and celebrations at home and church. And then on February 15, 1917, *The Chief* noted that "William Graves has been real sick the past week. He was not able to attend high school last week and isn't able at this writing to go back to school this week."[26] A few days later he was dead of pneumonia.

When the family realized he was dying, each sibling went in one at a time to say farewell. Grammie's voice broke when she told this to me. I was only 10 years old or so, but understood that she was still grieving her younger brother, dead for some 50 years at the time. The students and teachers at Troy High School were "terribly shocked" by his sudden death, and his freshman class gave flowers and went over as a body to his funeral. The obituary noted that he had planned to go to college after his graduation, and study for the ministry. "And as you look on the empty seat that he sat in in the assembly room," *The Chief* concluded, "you will remember that a student sat there who was one of the brightest and best pupils that Troy high [sic] school [sic] ever claimed as its own."[27]

Grandma saved a picture William had made of boys and girls ice skating on a pond, and had it framed and hung where she could look at it every day in the kitchen. As I remember it now, I am reminded of Grandma Moses and her American primitive paintings. I don't know what happened to it after my grandfather died and my aunt cleared out the house; she may have tossed it out or given it away. Or perhaps it was sold at the estate sale, and hangs in another house, with William's story forgotten.

Grammie also saved her grandfather James Etherton's manuscript, written in pencil on the "Improved Uniform Writing Paper Tablet Perfect For School, Home, and Office," and carefully noted his regiment and rank on a cover sheet in her neat handwriting.

She tucked it away with a portrait of James and his family and passed it on to her son, Lowell. I was puzzled years later after my uncle shared the manuscript with me that James would return to a place where he would not be welcomed. *Why didn't he just go west in the first place*, I wondered. Uncle Lowell wasn't sure, but thought perhaps because it was still home, and that James wanted to see his mother again. James died in 1906, and is buried in Mount Olive Cemetery in Troy, not far from Isaac Graves and John Kotsch—and his grandson William, and William's parents, David and Arria.

7

The Family Begins to Grow

Lura and Irving had a short courtship; they were married just three months later on April 14, 1921, at her parents' house in Troy. "A very impressive ceremony," declared *The Kansas Chief*.[1] Lura's older sister, Nellie, and Irving's brother, Arthur, preceded them into the living room to the strains of the Lohengrin wedding march performed on the piano by Ruth, the youngest of the Graves family. Lura wore hand-embroidered Georgette silk over white satin, and carried an arm bouquet of ferns and white roses. Irving was dressed in a suit of blue serge. In their wedding picture, Lura is smiling gently; she looks delicate and petite standing next to Irving, a tall, broad-shouldered young farmer.

After the wedding, O. R. and Mary went on an extended trip to Pennsylvania to visit her brother and then back to Chicago and Lockport to spend a few weeks with old friends and relatives. They did not return until just before Christmas. "Mr. Winkler reports Chicago as very damp," *The Montezuma Press* noted, and that "both seemed glad to get back to the clear air of southwest

Kansas."[2]

Irving and Lura, however, remained a few days in Troy, visiting Lura's friends and relatives, and then left for the farm. The Epworth League of the Methodist Church had been making plans for their arrival. The April social "was held at the O.R. Winkler home Tuesday night and was enjoyed by quite a large crowd, recorded *The Press* on the 29th. "The affair gave everyone quite an opportunity to meet and welcome Mr. and Mrs. Irving Winkler who were recently married. Refreshments of ice cream and cake were served."[3] Just a week later, on May 5, *The Press* noted "Quite a crowd charivaried [sic] Mr. and Mrs. Irving Winkler Monday night. Everyone reports a good time and plenty of noise."[4]

As Lura and Irving rode the train to Montezuma that April, she must have looked out the windows and watched the green, well-watered hills flatten out, and the trees grow far and few between, and then disappear entirely. It was surely a shock for her when she saw the dry, flat southwest corner, but she gamely settled in. My grandmother did her best to soften the harsh landscape, starting some geraniums in the kitchen window in order to provide some color, but when she transferred them outside, the relentless sun burned them, and the wind shredded the leaves.

Long after my grandmother had left the farm, I was surprised to discover a frilly tulip leaf poking up from under one of the elm trees one spring morning. Mom had not planted any, and we could only assume it was one planted by Grammie, and still struggling to grow and bloom after being dormant for so many years. We watered it, but one leaf was all it could manage. It would appear off and on over the years as I grew up, and once produced a flower, but eventually it disappeared.

I think that my grandmother must have been a little overwhelmed by her new surroundings, and homesick for her family, for less than a month later, Nellie came out to spend the summer with her. Nellie didn't actually spend much time with Lura, Dad said, for whenever there was a free moment from housework and chores, Arthur showed up and took Nellie for drives around the countryside and convinced her of a future on the farm. They were married the following May in Troy; this time Lura and Irving preceded them into the family living room, as Ruth sang "Until" and played the wedding march once more. Great-Uncle Arthur bought out Mr. Sweeny's quarter section, built a five-room bungalow, and moved in with Great-Aunt Nellie, up the hill from their sister-in-law and brother-in-law.

Lura and Nellie's father and mother, David and Arria Graves, were tempted by their reports of flat, fertile land out west, and followed their daughters three years later to farm around Copeland, a town west of Montezuma, with the flattest land in Gray County. Even their brother Ernest followed and farmed along with his father.

Lura and Irving's first child—a son, Arland—was born May 3, 1923. The doctor was summoned from Montezuma to the farm for the birth. It turned out to be a difficult delivery, and unhappily, the doctor had been drinking, according to Uncle Lowell, and had forgotten the forceps. Someone—probably Uncle—was sent back to town to fetch them, a round trip of 14 miles. The baby was born alive but was apparently injured in some way. Many years later, Lura confided to her second son Lowell that his father Irving carried the baby in his arms much of the four days that Arland lived. His death devastated them.

A couple of weeks later the grieving parents would insert a sad notice in *The Montezuma Press*: "We wish to thank our friends and neighbors for their kindness shown us during the recent illness and death of our darling baby Arland Winkler."[5]

My Uncle Lowell—your great-uncle—was born in 1926; Riley, your grandfather, followed five years later in 1931, and their sister Shirley, four years later in 1935. Auntie and Uncle adopted a daughter, Arlen, in 1929.

I found Arland's tiny headstone one day while Dad and I were walking around Fairview Cemetery. *Who's that*, I asked; I'd never heard of a Winkler relative named Arland before, and we were the only Winklers I knew of in Gray County. Dad explained that it was his baby brother, born and died years before he himself was born. It was sad to me, but so long ago and far-away, that I

Carol Winkler Kotsch

didn't think about it very long. I went back to wandering around, looking at the other headstones, and finding family names I recognized.

I loved my Grammie dearly; Uncle Lowell said she had a great deal of empathy for others. She fussed over my brother and me and listened to all of our adventures on the farm. She knew that I loved to read and kept books of fairy tales on hand for me when I spent the night, and made sure that I got a new mystery each birthday and Christmas. She herself also loved to read, and when I tired of Aladdin, I rummaged through her shelves. There wasn't anything more exciting than the safe and chaste romances of Grace Livingston Hill and Emilie Loring and I soon tired of the formula plots.

Grandma loved music and the farm had a piano, possibly the only farmhouse in Gray County to have one during those years. Your grandpa learned to play the piano, too, as well as the French horn; Uncle Lowell and Aunt Shirley played the clarinet in school. She taught me how to play a scale when I was little, but mostly I just plunked away at the keys. In the afternoons, I could hear her quavering voice as she played and sang her favorite hymns.

I was always fond of her name, and wanted to pass it along to you, Laura, but your father thought the unusual spelling would cause problems later. I also liked the traditional version, as I loved reading about Laura Ingalls Wilder, and so we compromised.

O. R. and Mary moved to Montezuma early in June, 1922, just shortly after Arthur and Nellie married. O. R. was 55 now, and no longer able to farm with his sons. He became a fixture in town and a respected member of the community; their lives now revolved around Montezuma and its inhabitants, and the church. In the evenings they would listen to the radio—O. R. kept a list of his favorite programs next to it—and Mary would sit in the corner crocheting. Often, they sat in their screened porch and simply watched the cars go by. At bedtime, O. R. helped Mary comb out her hair.

They had left behind the Evangelical Church they belonged to in Lockport—the parish was dissolved in 1920 and the building

The Farm on the Wall

demolished[6]—and became members of the Methodist Church in Montezuma. I used to see their names on a wall plaque commemorating the founders each time I went up the stairs from Sunday School to join my parents in the main sanctuary for church service. The congregation knew they could expect a long prayer when it was O. R.'s turn to lead. Mary was a teacher for the Sunday School, and both of them went on church picnics or participated in parties for the children, planning games and "delightful" refreshments. They were devout Christians, Uncle Lowell said, who read the Bible together every morning and prayed kneeling on the floor.

In 1924, O. R. became marshal of Montezuma, and kept an eye on the town as he went on his daily walks. In April, he warned residents to stop throwing trash into the back alleys, and that all outhouses and stables should be cleaned at once and kept clean during the summer.[7] A month later he had to take a sterner tone in response to loose chickens scratching in yards and destroying gardens: "It has got to the stage where arrests must be made unless chickens are locked up."[8]

Though he could no longer do heavy farm work, O. R. managed a large garden behind the house in Montezuma. Vegetables grew for him like no one else; he was especially known for the celery he harvested, a difficult vegetable to raise. Grandpa described to me how O. R. would heap up the soil around the rows of celery in order to blanch it and reduce the bitter flavor. "O. R. Winkler brought a bunch of celery to the Press Office Wednesday morning that he had raised in his garden. It was the self-blanching variety and is as good as you can buy anywhere. The bunch, leaves and all, measured 34 inches, which shows that that is real celery."[9]

O. R. took his produce—peas, carrots, lettuce, and the pale celery—and drove his 1926 Model T to Dodge City, where he sold it to Gwinner's restaurant, across the street from Eckles' Department store. He had learned to drive without much trouble, Uncle Lowell said, and got along real well with his Model T. He could maneuver it through narrow alleyways, and parallel park it in the tightest space on the city streets of Dodge. It was a pretty basic model, though, and after riding in his sons' roomier 1928 Hudson Touring car, with its larger engine and more efficient heater, he began to think that perhaps it was time to drive something more up-to-date.

A Hudson was more car than O. R. really needed, but he liked the look of the new 1930 Ford models and decided that one of them would be his next car, after talking it over with his sons. There was just a slight hitch, though: the new Ford models, like the '28 Hudson, had transmissions very different from O. R.'s Model T. Instead of using a pedal on the floor to shift from low to high gear, there was now a lever to use. *Don't worry*, said his sons. *We'll show you what to do.*

It seemed best to practice out on the farm; Grandpa sat in the front seat next to his father, and Uncle was in the back. O. R. looked down in some confusion at the unfamiliar arrangement of pedals and levers in the Hudson and listened as his sons explained what each one was. The clutch, at least, was still on the far left, but the brake was no longer the first pedal on the right; that was now the accelerator, which used to be a lever on the steering column. The brake had moved to the middle where reverse used to be.

Uncle and Grandpa began to rattle off directions. *Turn on the gas valve, now push the timing lever up, pull the throttle down, turn the choke, push the clutch down with your left foot, hit the starter button with your right foot, let go of the choke, ease up on the throttle, now give it some gas!*

O. R. struggled to follow their instructions; the car lurched forward, and they were off in a shaky circle around the farmyard.

A little more gas, shouted Uncle. O. R. groped uncertainly with his foot and hit the clutch instead of the accelerator and the engine died. *No, no!* his sons chorused. *Try again.*

Once more O. R. went through the unfamiliar steps, and the Hudson went bouncing over the ruts.

Too much! yelled my grandpa.

Hit the brake! hollered Uncle.

O. R. pressed down hard, but not on the brake. He had hit the accelerator pedal instead and the car went even faster.

Stop! shouted his sons. *We're going to hit the barn!*

Thoroughly flustered and confused, O. R. reverted to the days of driving a horse and wagon.

Whoa, whoa there, whoaaa, Nellie! he bellowed, and leaned back and pulled on the steering wheel as he would have pulled on the reins. The car hit the side of the barn and the motor died.

In the silence, he got out of the car, looked his sons in the eye and declared, *That's it. No more.* He drove his outdated but dependable Model T back to town, leaving his sons to deal with the dents in their Hudson. He never got another car.

He was, by all accounts, a sober and rather stern man who spoke in a gruff voice, but he startled Dad and Uncle Lowell one day with an unexpected flash of humor. They had attended services with their parents at the Church of Christ one Sunday. As a treat afterwards, they were permitted to ride back to the farm for Sunday dinner with O. R. and Mary. As the Model T putt-putted along the dirt roads, O. R. turned a corner, and unexpectedly, without a word spoken between them, he and Mary exchanged their hats. The boys were astonished to see O. R.'s somber fedora hanging over Mary's ears, and Mary's flowery Sunday best perched on O. R.'s head. Then Mary started to giggle and everyone burst out laughing the rest of the way to the farm.

O. R. and Mary lived to celebrate their 50th wedding anniversary on November 25, 1940, surrounded by their children and grandchildren, and their siblings and in-laws. They and their guests were served a turkey dinner, courtesy of their Sunday School, and were entertained with a short talk from their minister, two violin solos from their granddaughter Arlen, and a vocal solo from a friend. The seventy friends and neighbors who called during the open house admired the four elaborate cakes prepared for the occasion by their daughters-in-law. *The Press* noted that while O. R. had not completely recovered from a recent illness, he enjoyed it all with no ill effects.[10]

O. R., though, was failing fast from stomach cancer. He died on March 16, 1941, my father's tenth birthday, and only a few months before the U.S. entered war against Germany for a second time. The church that was such a big part of his life could not accommodate all the mourners, and the funeral was held in the high school gym. "A man the community will miss greatly" read the headline in *The Press*.[11]

After O. R.'s death, Uncle Lowell used the Model T to drive back and forth to school for a couple of years—Mary had never learned to drive and the car was of no use to her. When he left for the service, the car stayed on the farm inside the long shed. By now it was long past its prime, but a neighbor, Russell Dirks, thought it was a fine old machine. He bought it, and hoisted the lightweight old auto up into the haymow of his own barn, intending to restore it. It sat there for some 20 years until Russell came home from church one Sunday to find his barn on fire. It was a total loss, and the car was gone.

While Mary would walk to church and the grocery store in Montezuma on her own, Grandpa and Uncle saw to their mother's care, driving her to Dodge City to the doctor, and making sure the house was in good order. She died in 1950 and was buried next to O. R. in Fairview Cemetery; the railroad that brought them to Kansas is just a few miles away.

8

Harvesting Wheat and Dust

The Irving Winklers at the bottom of the hill and the Arthur Winklers up the hill shared one truck, one car, one checkbook, and one bank account. Together Grandpa and Uncle worked the fields of the two farms, planting wheat as the cash crop, and dry land milo and barley to feed the milk cows and the workhorses, as well as the chickens and hogs. Grandma and Auntie took care of their homes, cooking, sewing, cleaning, and raising vegetables and chickens.

Grandpa and Uncle and their father had started out with just three or four horses but added more to keep up with the demands of farming. The 10 to 12 hardworking horses that plowed and harvested had to be shod on a regular basis, which was Uncle's job; he was always good with his hands. A little forge stood behind the granary where the seed wheat was stored. You can see it still in the picture of the farm. The contents were salvaged, and the building torn down while I was quite young, but I remember seeing the heavy iron anvil where Uncle once hammered out horseshoes, using the tools I saw hanging in the little shed. I found a lump of lead in there before it was torn down and added it to my rock collection. Your grandfather still has the anvil.

The men would plow the gardens up the hill and down the hill each spring, but Grandma and Auntie did the rest, planting and weeding, and canning the vegetables. Grandpa had a taste for tartness, so they put in a rhubarb patch at the bottom of the hill. It grew large, floppy, triangular leaves on top of stalks that were crisp and green like celery, but ruby-red at the base. Grandma added lots of sugar when she chopped the stalks into pieces and covered them with piecrust. They also put in an asparagus bed for something green early in the spring. There was a frame for cucumbers, a tent-shaped trellis which supported the vines. I remember creeping under it when I was little; it made a fine, shady house. The cucumbers were turned into pickles; the rows of cabbage became sauerkraut.

One day while hoeing in the garden, my tiny grandmother discovered a rattler lurking among the rows. The men were out in the field, and she knew she would have to take care of it herself. She raised the hoe slowly and cautiously, so as not to startle the snake into striking, and then swung with all her might. The force of the blow was so hard that it sent her flying up into the air. Grandma swung the hoe again and again, screaming each time she brought it down, until the snake was in tatters. When she realized it was dead, she carried it over to the field and buried it, and shakily went back to hoeing the rest of the garden.

The two sisters quickly immersed themselves into the religious and social life available in Montezuma. Their Washington ancestors—through George's aunt Anne—were likely Anglican, but that changed when Sarah Elsberry married Baptist preacher John Riley. In Troy, they had grown up in the Baptist Church; their grandfather Isaac Graves had been one of the founding members. The closest equivalent now was the Church of Christ, which held services in the Legion Hall. Brother Ernest became superintendent. The Christian Church News which appeared in *The Press* on September 17, 1931, reported the Sunday sermon was "Three

Fold Mission of Jesus," and that a quartet of Iris and Opal Woods, and Nellie and Lura Winkler sang "He's a Wonderful Saviour [sic] to Me." Both families were active members, attending Christian Endeavor Rallies, or prohibition meetings.

Lura and Nellie were an integral part of the Christian Ladies Aid, frequently hosting meetings at the two farms. If the meetings were held in town, the sisters would drive the family car while the men were in the fields. The Ladies Aid members met to sew or quilt for the poor, but equally important was the chance to sing and play the piano and give readings as they had done in Troy. Afterwards, the ladies had a social hour and discussed the refreshments and the goings-on in town.

Their names—and Mary's—also show up in meetings of the Home Culture Club, the Study Club, and the Sorosis Club. They listened to talks about home and family, meal preparation, and sewing. "Something New for My Garden," was the topic for the January 1933 meeting of the Home Culture Club. Once again there was a social hour with cake and punch, or wafers and iced tea. Then it was back to the farm in time to prepare supper for the men.

In the fall Grandpa and Uncle hitched up the team to the drill and planted about 300 acres of the all-important winter wheat. After that, it was a gamble that there would be enough moisture to sprout the wheat, that winter winds wouldn't dry out the tender blades, that gentle rains instead of heavy thunderstorms and hail would arrive in the spring, and that leaf rust and aphids would not infest the fields.

The soil in Winkler half section—and in Gray County—was indeed as deep and rich as described by F. M. Luther, and well suited for dry land wheat farming, especially for the winter wheat that had been introduced by pacifist Mennonite settlers in 1874. While living in Russia during the nineteenth century, to escape religious persecution and military conscription in Germany, they had discovered from Turkish farmers in the Crimea that wheat could be planted in the fall, sprout, and then lie dormant all winter. When the snow melted, it would surge into life again in time to take advantage of spring rains. The early harvest in June meant the crop would avoid not only the dry heat of summer, but blights and bugs as well. This was the story that I—along with most Kansans learned—that Mennonite children were set to work picking out only the best grains from the harvest to take with them to America. There was a little more to it, however.

When changeable czars threatened their religious freedom in Russia, the Mennonites settled in Kansas in 1873-74, to find that corn dominated the area, a grain they were unfamiliar with. They may indeed have brought some of the wheat they grew in Russia with them and planted it in small plots, but testimony from early settlers shows they also purchased wheat in Kansas, and railroad officials provided discounted seed wheat to them—probably Early Red May, a soft red spring wheat.[1]

Indeed, most of the wheat grown in Kansas prior to 1873 was soft spring wheat, as the population preferred flour from soft wheat. Besides, the local mills were not able to effectively grind the hard berries of Turkey Red. But then a change in immigration patterns in the early 1880s led to a demand for hard red winter wheat over soft spring wheat. New arrivals from southern and eastern Europe were used to leavened breads made with flour from hard wheat high in protein and gluten.[2] In response, agricultural agents began experimenting with several different types of hard wheat from Russia.

Bernhard Warkentin, a Mennonite miller's son who had emigrated from the Ukrainian area in 1872 and eventually settled in Newton, returned to the Crimea in 1885-6, and brought back several other samples of hard red wheat, and pioneered the further testing of these samples.[3] These hard red wheat varieties had greater hardiness and were more resistant to winter kill and black rust.[4] Warkentin had already adapted his own mill in Newton with steel roller machinery that could make fine flour out of the hard berries, and encouraged other mills in Kansas to do the same. The advantages were obvious, and it didn't take long for hard winter wheat to spread across Kansas—and to Oklahoma, Texas, Colorado and Nebraska; by 1909, corn was in second place.[5]

The Farm on the Wall

Anxiously, Grandpa and Uncle watched their wheat shoot up in spring, head out in May, and turn from green to gold. In June, they tested the kernels daily to see how they were forming. When the kernels were almost, but not quite ripe, then it was time to cut. If they waited until the wheat was fully dry and ripe, then the kernels would shatter onto the ground as the wheat was being cut.

The brothers could not harvest on their own. They hired two or three men to help them run the header, and pull the wagons, and stack the wheat. Uncle hitched up the four workhorses to push the header; if they pulled it, they would trample the grain in front of them as they walked along. Uncle stood on the platform of the three-wheeled header, guiding the horses. Attached to the platform was the reel, which pulled the wheat backwards, and a sickle that cut the stalks about six to eight inches below the head. If the wheat was tall that year, Uncle would raise the platform so there wouldn't be as much excess straw for the thresher. If the fields were wet, Uncle or Grandpa would have to work hard to keep the horses in line as they struggled through the mud. Sometimes Grandpa would continue yelling at the horses in his sleep, waking my startled grandmother.

The stalks and heads dropped onto a canvas belt about four feet wide, which conveyed the wheat up and over and down into the header barge, a large, four-wheeled wagon, that Grandpa was driving right alongside the header. He had to make sure his team kept pace with Uncle's horses, so that the barge stayed even with the wheat dropping out of the chute; otherwise, it would fall to the ground. Inside the header barge, one of the hired men spread the wheat evenly to every corner so it didn't all pile up in one place.

When Grandpa's barge was full, he turned his team aside to the stacking ground, while a second header barge took his place alongside the header. The hired man pitched the wheat over the side of barge onto the ground, and Grandpa shaped it as it piled higher and higher, so any rain would run off and not soak into the stack. By now, the second barge was full and ready to unload, and Grandpa swung his team and empty barge back alongside the header for another round.

Carol Winkler Kotsch

On a good day, they could cut perhaps a total of 30 to 35 acres. At noontime, Grandma and Auntie brought them cool water and fed them dinner while horses were switched and rested. Then the men changed jobs, though Uncle usually stayed on the header as they began cutting again; he was always good with horses. They ended up with two or three stacks to thresh, depending on how much rain had fallen that spring. When they finished, the horses were unharnessed, and the header and the barges parked to one side. The stacked wheat sat under the hot sun and finished ripening.

At the end of July, it was time to separate the kernels from the heads. For that they needed a threshing machine, an expensive piece of technology. A neighbor to the west, Henry X. Smith, had bought one, and traveled with it to area farms, where for a fee, he would run the wheat through his thresher. Henry and his crew pulled the threshing machine behind their tractor when they arrived at the Winkler farm, stopping right between the haystacks.

The thresher was not self-powered; it was run by a belt attached to the tractor engine which was stretched to a pulley on the thresher. One man ran the threshing machine, while two others pitched the wheat on the bundle feeder, drawing it inside the cylinder and tumbling it around and around until the grain fell to the bottom and the chaff and dust were blown out.[6] Another man stacked up the straw as it was ejected; it was saved and used as bedding for the Winkler livestock. The grain poured out the other end into Grandpa's wagon. It would be stored on the farm and hauled into town later.

It took about two days to thresh the Winkler crop, Dad thought, and then Henry X. and his crew would move onto another farmer's harvest. In the meantime, Grammie and Auntie were working constantly in the kitchen and the farmyard to feed the hungry, hardworking crew of eight or nine men. In the morning, they would butcher and clean several chickens they had raised from chicks and fry them up. Vegetables were scrubbed, peeled, and boiled, bread kneaded and baked, and pie crusts rolled out and filled. The local farmwives all tried to out-do one another in feeding the harvesters, and Grammie and Auntie saw to it that none of the hands went away hungry.

Henry X. was a member of the Church of God in Christ Mennonite, a pacifist Protestant sect that preached literal interpretation of the scriptures and strict adherence to church law. Members were required to live simple lives without modern conveniences, so Henry was somewhat of an anomaly with his threshing machine, but the church elders permitted it.

They were easy to identify in our small farm community; indeed, they made up the majority of the population. The men wore beards and the women covered their hair with small black caps to keep them from becoming vain. Unlike the Amish, the Mennonites I knew used zippers, but all their clothing was plain and unadorned, though the women varied their cookie-cutter dresses with different colors. They drove only plain, single-color cars, and took out the radios after they bought them from the dealer. The men were either farmers or carpenters, a vocation permitted since Jesus was a carpenter himself.

Their fundamentalist beliefs and plain living meant that they did not mix easily with the rest of the population in Gray County. Though we lived and worked next to each other, and shopped at the same stores in town, and went to school together, we did not socialize with them, aside from a chat in the field, or trading help on the farm. Sometimes I would hear the older Mennonite ladies speaking in Low German at the A. G. when we went shopping for groceries.

I could not understand why Mennonites rejected so many things the rest of the world casually accepted, such as dinosaurs and television. On Sundays, when we picked up the newspaper at the post office after church, we would find the trash can stuffed with the funny papers that devout Mennonite families had removed, lest they be tempted into idle reading. The girls could not run around in shorts and jeans as I did, or ride horses, or go swimming. It seemed a very boring sort of life to me, and I felt sorry for them, until I discovered that they considered my activities sinful.

Carol Winkler Kotsch

Despite the differences in our beliefs, they were good neighbors, coming to the aid of believers and non-believers alike, whether it was helping Dad find strayed cattle, or rushing to help in areas hit by tornadoes or floods. Grandpa and Uncle worked well enough alongside of them for years, as did my father, but cigar-smoking, whiskey-sipping great-Uncle Lloyd was another story.

The Winkler Brothers were threshing wheat on the farm one year with Henry X's crew, when Uncle Lloyd asked one of the Mennonite men why they all wore beards.

Why, to look like Jesus, or as close as we can, he replied.

Look like Jesus! whooped Great-Uncle Lloyd as he eyed the long, bushy beard in disbelief. *By God, you look like the devil to me!*

In the late 1920s, threshing machines were replaced by combines that not only cut the wheat from the stalks, but also removed the grain from the heads. This machine was still pulled by a tractor; Grandpa and Uncle bought a Rumely to pull their combine. In the late 1940s self-propelled combines were developed and large crews to finish the harvest were a thing of the past. The horses were no longer needed, and Uncle then turned to repairing machinery. One day, while looking at the ripening wheat, I asked my father how big an acre was, trying to picture my Grandpa and Uncle harvesting. Dad told me it was a bit smaller than the football field at the high school in town. The last combine he owned could cut over 100 acres a day.

When the Great War was over, demand for wheat dropped, and so did prices. Even more grassland was plowed up and planted to wheat in order to make the same amount of money. Horse-drawn plows were still used, but now gasoline-powered tractors pulling new one-way disc plows to pulverize the topsoil into fine dirt were taking their place, more efficient but expensive machinery that had to be paid for. The Roaring Twenties encouraged consumerism and credit-based borrowing, but as the wheat kept right on growing year after year, not many had worried about payments.

The Farm on the Wall

In the mid-to-late 1920s, Grandpa and Uncle had raised several good wheat crops in a row and were feeling flush with some extra money. P. T. Harvey, a prominent farmer in Gray County, had bought some land in southeast Colorado, and Grandpa and Uncle decided to follow his example. They bought some ground in Bacca County, land very similar to southwest Kansas, and rented it out. The tenant and his family lived in an existing house on the property and were to provide the Winkler Brothers with a share of the wheat harvest.

They didn't hear anything from their tenant after the wheat was cut, let alone receive a share of the harvest. Grandpa and Uncle decided to drive out and take a look for themselves. As they got closer to their property, they stopped at a little grain elevator to see if any wheat had been stored under their name. *Nothing here*, the manager told them. *Try the next one.* They received the same answer at the next elevator. *Try the one in Springfield*, they were told. *It's probably there.*

But it wasn't. They drove out to their ground, and found the fields cut, and the house cleaned out and completely empty. All that was left of their wheat crop was a five-foot pipe wrench. They could not trace their tenant. There was nothing for it but to rent it out again to another tenant, who proved to be more reliable. Grandpa and Uncle eventually sold the property to him and his son but kept the pipe wrench. They didn't like to talk about the incident, Dad remembered. The wrench was used for heavy jobs around the farm for many years until my father sold it at his farm sale.

In 1931, the year my father was born, Grandpa and Uncle raised one of the largest crops they had ever seen, thanks to abundant rain and snow during the previous fall and winter, but the price per bushel was only a quarter now. They decided to store it in the granary on the farm and hope that prices would go higher. Some of their neighbors decided to store their grain in the elevator at Montezuma but had to pay to do so.

The rains were less the next year, and they raised an average crop, but the price had dropped to ten cents a bushel. Grandpa and Uncle continued storing it on the farm and sold some if the price went up, or if they needed money, but many farmers were forced to sell their entire crop before storage fees ate up all the profits. Soon, Grandpa and Uncle learned to take a different route to town when they had wheat to sell, to avoid talk from envious neighbors.

And then the rains stopped. A periodic drought had settled over the prairie, worse than previous ones, which were forgotten when the rains returned. Indeed, early promoters, who had only seen a wet cycle, declared there was plenty of rainfall.[7]

> "The history of the west," wrote F. M. Luther, "has proven conclusively that the breaking up of the virgin soil tends to equalize the atmospheric moisture, as the broken and loose soil forms a huge sponge which gives off the vapor slowly instead of allowing it to evaporate quickly as it would when poured upon the hard sod...and as it is more and more becoming farmed each year, the rainfall becomes more equalized and conditions more and more favorable."[8]

The jet stream that normally flowed west over the Gulf of Mexico, and then turned north, pulling up moisture, weakened, and the plains dried. Summers became hotter, with temperatures in the hundreds day after day after day, setting records during the next several years that still stand. Alton and Fredonia, Kansas, reached a high of 121° on July 24, 1936.

The natural grass cover that had kept the soil in place and prevented moisture from evaporating was gone, replaced by crops that were now withering and exposing bare ground. "At that time, the smoother the field, the better the farmer," remembered Inez Unruh, daughter of neighbors to the south, "so the fields were wide open and took to the skies."[9] The always constant winds blew harder now, raising a little dust at first, and then more and more. It drifted like snow, choking animals and people alike. Red dust storms came from Oklahoma, gray from Colorado, and black clouds originated from Kansas.

Finally, a massive storm occurred on April 14, 1935, which gave the Dust Bowl its name. Like many other dust storms it started on the northern end of the plains, in the Dakotas, and then swept south across Wyoming, Colorado, Kansas, Oklahoma and Texas, carrying with it over 300,000 tons of topsoil.[10] It blocked the sun as it rolled over the country, and temperatures plummeted 50 degrees; soil dropped over Chicago, Pittsburg and New York, even out to ships at sea.

On the farm, they had noticed some dust blowing that day, but they didn't see the roll of black clouds moving in from the northwest. Uncle Lowell and Grandpa were in the kitchen when at about two in the afternoon, it went absolutely black, and Uncle Lowell could not see his father across the room. They lit the kerosene lamp, and gradually it got lighter. Black Sunday, it was called afterwards, and led a reporter back east to refer to "the dust bowl of the continent."[11] Southwest Kansas and the Oklahoma Panhandle were the areas hardest hit of the Great Plains.

Dark clouds rolled in like a weather front almost every day, Uncle Lowell said, but instead of rain, they blew in dust so thick that the students at his one-room school stayed inside for noon recess. At home, if Grandpa noticed black clouds moving in, he would race out to put the chickens and cows in the barn, to keep them from breathing in the dust and developing pneumonia. Dad and Uncle Lowell would help Grandma hang wet sheets over the door and windows. In the morning they would be brown with dust. In town, members of the Methodist Church would climb up into the church attic with shovels and scoop out the dust that had seeped in so the ceiling wouldn't collapse.

The storms scoured away the ground cover on the fields, blowing out the soil and leaving behind bare patches, which would grow larger and larger. Farmers worked the fields to bring up large chunks of soil that would not blow, but the dry weather continued. Some rain did fall, but not enough to produce good crops; only a dusting of snow fell during the winter. Wheat that managed to grow in 1936 was eaten by a plague of grasshoppers in some areas. One year, Grandpa did not take the combine out of the shed. There was no wheat in the fields to cut.

Despite the poor rainfall and the blowing dust, the Winkler Brothers usually managed to harvest something during the Dirty Thirties. Uncle Lowell began helping in the fields when he was about eight years old. At harvest time, he would drive the tractor that pulled the combine around and around the field in ever decreasing squares, while Grandpa stood on the platform of the combine, raising and lowering the header to match the height of the wheat.

When Uncle Lowell reached the end the field, though, he wasn't strong enough to turn the tractor around the corner. He turned off the switch to stop the tractor, while Grandpa jumped down from the combine, ran to the tractor, turned the corner and ran back to the combine. It was a light harvest during those dry years, and it took a long time to fill the grain bin on the combine. Then the grain was unloaded onto a truck and Uncle drove it back to the farm where it was stored in the granary for six months, or up to five years, depending on the market price.

The stock market crash of '29 hadn't affected the farmers immediately, but now they felt it. When Uncle Lowell was about seven or eight years old, he began to notice the hardships. Overalls were patched and re-patched. To make shoes wear longer, Grandpa turned them upside-down on the shoemaker's last, and hammered on new soles and heels from Duckwall's Variety Store in Dodge City. If the car or truck broke down, Grandpa and Uncle repaired them as best they could, as they could not afford to take them to the garage in town.

Peering into the window of Duckwall's one day, when he was about five or six, Dad spied a little die-cast model of a John Deere tractor that was priced for a quarter. He fingered the dime and nickel he had in his pocket and asked his mother if he could have another dime. She went through her purse, checking to see how much money she had. Then she closed her eyes and calculated how much she would need to buy groceries and clothes. After a long pause, she closed the purse with a sigh. *I can't spare a dime*, she told Dad.

It was the milk and cream that kept them going, Dad remembered, and what they could grow in the garden. Every day, Grandma and Auntie gathered eggs, cleaned them, and packed them downstairs in egg cases that held 30 dozen eggs when full. Grandpa and Uncle milked the cows by hand each day—about five or six, Uncle Lowell said—once in the morning, and again in the evening. They balanced on a t-shaped milking stool instead of a three- or four-legged stool; Dad thought it was easier to pick up as they moved from cow to cow. The cream was strained off in the separator and poured into a five-gallon milk can and stored in the cool milk house as well. The two families drank the rest of the milk or made cottage cheese from it; anything left over from that was fed to the pigs.

On Saturday mornings, they took the cream and eggs into town. The eggs were sold in Montezuma, but the cream went by train to Dodge City to Fairmont Foods, which had a creamery, a chicken hatchery, and which also trucked produce over several states. Grandpa watched the cream prices, though, and he would switch to Newton or Hutchinson, if they were paying more. The cream can carried a tag with "Winkler Brothers" stamped on it so the creamery would know whom to credit, and the cans were shipped back to Montezuma where Grandpa picked them up at the train depot.

The hard times meant that treats were far and few between when Dad and Uncle Lowell were growing up during the 1930s, but one year at Christmas, Grandpa saw an advertisement in *The Montezuma Press*, a special offer for a two-pound box of chocolates from a Kansas City store. He ordered it, and it was shipped out by train, but when Grandpa opened the box, the chocolates were smashed and broken.

Indignantly, he sat down and wrote a letter to the company, which unexpectedly shipped another two-pound box free of charge, and which arrived in better condition. In the evening after supper, the family lined up while Grandpa doled out one chocolate to each person and made it last as long as possible.

Carol Winkler Kotsch

Christmastime also meant that Grandma would make raisin bread and hot chocolate for breakfast before they opened gifts, something Dad and Uncle Lowell waited for eagerly. It became a Christmas tradition that Uncle Lowell carried on in his own family. When I passed along the story to you, girls, you were amazed that something as ordinary and commonplace as raisin bread and hot chocolate would be considered a special treat. But so it was to your grandpa in those days, and he looked forward to it.

The dust and wind blew on and on, year after year; the price of wheat stayed low. *We've got to do something*, Grandma told Grandpa one day; *it isn't any good staying here.* Grandpa paused a long time and said *Lura—it isn't any better anywhere else; if we sold the farm it wouldn't be enough to buy more land elsewhere. Besides—who else can buy it?* They stuck it out.

But not everyone could hang on as my grandparents did. When farmers could not pay back what they had borrowed, the banks foreclosed. Houses were simply abandoned as families loaded up and went looking for work, some to nearby towns, or the oil fields of the region, and others farther west to California. Morton County, in the very corner of southwest Kansas, lost 47 percent of its population.[12]

The drought and dust storms continued until about 1937, when rain finally returned. The next year, when Uncle Lowell was 12, he was able to turn the corners on his own while driving the tractor, but the rains had been so heavy, that for the first time he could ever remember, they harvested in the mud.

9

Mining Boom and Bust

The Winkler Brothers had been a formal partnership since 1922, but Grandpa and Uncle had been working together from the time they were boys on their grandparent's farm in Lockport. It all ended in the spring of 1947 when Grandpa and Uncle and Dad drove to Copeland to pick up some tractor parts at the implement dealer. The ones they needed were stored in a loft up above the rest of the office, and for some reason, Uncle himself climbed the ladder to get them. The ladder slipped and Uncle landed on the concrete floor, breaking his back. It healed after time, but he could no longer do the hard, physical work on the farm. He and Auntie retired and moved to Dodge City a year later in the spring of 1948, leaving Grandpa somewhat lost after all their years together. The house up the hill, the "little bungalow" that Uncle built when he and Auntie married, was rented out.

The wheat still had to be cut, though, the fields plowed, and the cattle fed, but now it was just Grandpa and my father, who worked with Grandpa through high school and beyond. Uncle

The Farm on the Wall

Lowell had finished his stint in the service after WWII and was putting himself through college. Farming suited your grandpa; Uncle Lowell remembered how his mother would keep an eye on Dad out the kitchen window as he played with his toy tractors and plows in a little farm scratched out on the ground.

Dad met my mother—your grandmother—in Dodge City, where he and his buddies made frequent trips at the end of a hard week. One evening, after they had finished a movie, and worked up a sweat roller-skating, they headed west on Wyatt Earp Boulevard to Kline's Dairy for a milkshake. It was an ice cream parlor that also sold sandwiches, and it was the place to go, Dad said, where you could see, and be seen. Like the nearby Toot and Tell 'Em, you pulled into the parking lot, honked your horn, flashed your headlights, and a carhop appeared to take your order.

On this particular night the lot was full up, and Dad had parked too far away for the carhops. He went inside to place his order, and when he looked up to take his change, he found himself quite taken with the blue-eyed, dark-haired young lady on the other side of the counter. Jacqueline Dugan—she went by Jackie—was a city girl but knew something about horses.

Mom's family was from the lead and zinc mining community of Galena in the southeast corner of Kansas. She didn't have any stories about her family and hadn't like studying history in school. The *past is past*, she once declared as we were driving home from a shopping trip in Dodge. *It's over and done with and you can't change it.*

But it's more than memorizing facts and dates, I tried to explain. *The past is still shaping the present, and if we understand how and why things happened, then we are better prepared not to make the same mistakes.* I was a very earnest young college student, full of newly-acquired knowledge, but little experience and understanding. Mom had seen a lot more of the world than I had, and she didn't reply, thinking maybe, of people who had made the same choices over and over, and learned nothing from them.

Nor can I remember hearing any stories from her parents. It

Carol Winkler Kotsch

wasn't until after her mother died, that Mom received a family history of the Dugans. I read through it and was absorbed by the story of Erastus Dugan, her great-grandfather, whose unusual first name was a Latin version of the Greek word for "beloved." Namesakes went by "Ross." The stories were compiled by a Dugan great-aunt of hers, Evalina Fields Gasswint. She wrote, "I do have a desire to pass on knowledge from tale, [sic] life and research, and beg forgiveness if it is incorrect. The quotations will be from books, my mother's story [sic] and people."

Sometime after he was widowed, Erastus moved in with his daughter, Harriet, and her husband, William Fields, in Sheridan, Oklahoma.

> "He was a large-framed man," Evalina wrote, "had thin white hair, a long beard, and I'll always remember his pink, bald head. My mother always took pride in washing him as his pipe discolored his beard. He was a humerous [sic] old chap, sitting in his rocker, with his newspaper and his pipe, swatting flies and chatting about politics and humming some diddle tune, keeping time with his hands and feet. He could play some tunes very well such as 'Old Dan Tucker' and 'The Irish Washer Woman.'"

His grandfather was an Irish immigrant by the name of William Patrick Dugan, born about 1755. According to pension records, he was a private in the 3rd New Jersey Regiment and fought in the Battles of Brandywine, Germantown, and Monmouth of the Revolutionary War. He married Jane Adams, and they ended up in Kentucky, where son and daughter John and Jane were born in 1800. From Kentucky, they moved to Ohio, where a second son, Ross, was born.

There William and his family fell upon hard times. In 1818, he applied to a recent act of Congress to "provide for certain persons engaged in the land and naval service of the United States in the revolutionary war," swearing that "he is very infirm and unable to perform any work of account and that he cannot support himself without the aid of the government or public or private charity and that his wife and children are unable to render him much assistance." Among his assets he listed a brick oven, a pot, some forks, a bed and bedding, and one old ax. He subsequently received $8 a month for his service. In his later years, the townspeople referred to him as "Major," and in 1901 local historian Frazer Wilson prodded local authorities to move William's remains to a soldiers' plot in the new cemetery.

Named after his father's brother, Erastus was born on January 16, 1837, in Darke County, Ohio. He was the fourth of nine children born to John Dugan and Eliza Tullis. When he was old enough, probably in his late teens, he and a friend went west as Indian scouts. "At one place they rode almost to the top of a high hill, tied their horses and walked on so they could see the valley. There was an Indian settlement of many teepees and a line where women's and children's scalps were drying."

He kept going west, ending up in San Francisco where he enlisted with the 2nd Regiment California Volunteer Cavalry Company M in September of 1861, just after President Lincoln's second call upon the state for troops in August. Evalina thought he must have been attracted to California by stories of the gold rush, as he listed his occupation as a miner on the enlistment paper.

By October 30, 1861, the regiment was organized, and company M was stationed at Camp Alert. From there Erastus and the rest of the company rode all about the west, from one military fort to the next, surveying roads, fighting Indians and protecting mail routes. He was stationed and saw action at some of the Old West's most famous names: Fort Bridger, Fort Laramie, Spanish Fork Canyon, and the Bear River Massacre.

After a three-year hitch, he was discharged on October 4, 1865, from Camp Douglas in Utah, and from there he rode back home to Lincoln, Illinois, where his family had moved in the meantime. Evalina wrote that her grandfather "killed crows for food, drank water from streams, and had a leg sore caused by the saddle."

Evalina didn't know how long it took Erastus to reach Illinois, but on January 15, 1865, he married Caroline Etterlein, a

Carol Winkler Kotsch

daughter of German immigrants. Her alcoholic father, Oscar—or John—the records differ—had deserted her mother, also named Caroline, and her brothers, William and John. As the oldest, she hired herself out to work for other families. She was hardly 15 years old when she met Erastus, but she recognized him as a stable, dependable man and accepted his offer of marriage.

Erastus and his new bride then headed west again, but this time to Kansas. It must have been in late winter or early spring, as the Missouri River was iced over at Kansas City when they crossed, and then they rode the stagecoach south to Fort Scott. There Caroline rested from the ride in a rocking chair; the chair's owner charged them a dollar for one hour.

After his years of mining and soldiering, Erastus was ready to settle down and farm. Just eight miles southeast from Fort Scott they purchased some land and began to plow. Alva, my mother's grandfather, was born there in 1867, the first of their eleven children. In just a few years, though, they pulled up stakes and moved to another farm, a scenario they followed several times, though they stayed in Bourbon County. Each farm was better than the last, Evalina wrote, though the family had to work hard to keep themselves fed.

> Alva plowed sod with an oxen team. They picked wild fruit, butchered enough pork to fill a barrel, rendered fat for lard and soap. They could buy green coffee which Grandma (Caroline) roasted in the oven and ground in a coffee grinder, then stored in a container. They had a large basement for storage of fruit, a barrel of kraut and a barrel of cucumbers in salt to be soaked later and put in homemade vinegar. Grandpa (Erastus) made sorghum for the home. Grandma had her thimble finger caught in the cane mill, as my mother (Harriet) ran in front of the old gray horse. There was no anesthetic, so she (Caroline) sat on Grandpa's lap while the doctor amputated the finger. This was before Aunt Kate was born. Molasses was used instead of sugar in making vinegar, fruit butters, cakes and

The Farm on the Wall

many other ways. The children picked blackberries by the boiler full and they didn't have chigger medicine. They raised potatoes by the wagon load and drove into the pond to wash them before they were dried and stored.

They walked one and one-half miles to Rocky Vale, a one-room ungraded school of usually 35 students of all ages. Children worked at home and went to school barefoot. My mother (Harriet) said she studied grammar one month. They had a six-month term but the girls had all the fall work to do before starting, such as raking the yard, beating out two bushel sacks of navy beans and storing potatoes down in the cellar. They dried 50-pound sacks of sweet corn as they did not can. Grandpa would take shelled corn to the grist mill to grind for cornmeal.

Though family members may have looked back fondly on those early days, it was hard work and it didn't pay very well. It was hilly country, Dad told me, with thin, rocky soil, and better suited for cattle. Alva, the oldest son of Erastus and Caroline, became a blacksmith, and when the lead and zinc boom started in Galena not far off, he became an engineer in the mines, eventually ending up as a mill foreman. His son, Jack, my grandfather, would follow him into the mines, becoming a tractor driver for the Eagle-Picher lead smelter in Galena. Jack married Bessie Julia Belle Derfelt, daughter and granddaughter of miners, on February 19, 1935. My mother, Jacqueline, was born in October; a sister followed two years later.

Lumps of lead had been picked up at the surface for years in the southeast corner of Kansas, and in 1877 nearby mining companies in Missouri starting buying up lots in order to mine the rich veins of lead and zinc that were buried about 200 feet below the surface in the tri-state area of Kansas, Oklahoma, and Missouri. This 2,500 square mile region would eventually produce about 50 percent of all the zinc and 10 percent of all lead mined in the entire United States.[1] In Cherokee County, Kansas, Galena and Empire City sprang up cheek-by-jowl overnight and fought over the ore that ran through both locations. Doctors and undertakers worked overtime in the violent boomtown once saloons and gambling lured miners out of their hard-earned wages.

Some strip mining was done in Cherokee County, but most of the mining was done underground. "Large room-shaped areas were mined out, and similarly shaped areas were left for roof support, resulting in a checkerboard-like arrangement of alternating rooms and pillars. Underground rooms had walls 25 to 100 feet high and pillars 20 to 50 feet thick. In the eastern part of the district, however, the ore was closer to the surface, and the shallow mining could be done using hand tools and a simple hoisting device that was either man- or animal-powered. Galena became known as a poor man's mining district because small claims could be worked by a few miners."[2]

Nearly the entire area was hollowed out, and even the areas left for roof support were mined in search of more minerals. It was said trucks could drive from one mine to another underground, though the clearance might only be a few inches on either side of some of the tunnels. The water table was high in the area, and when the mines closed in the seventies, they flooded, and boats could be floated through the abandoned caverns.

During the mining heyday in the 1920s, "more than 11,000 miners worked in the area, and perhaps three times as many were involved in support work and industries."[3] Out of approximately 115 million tons of mined ore, the mining towns of Cherokee County—Galena, Baxter Springs, and Treece—produced 2.9 million tons of zinc worth about $436 million, and 650,000 tons of lead worth nearly $91 million.[4] The discarded rubble—chat—was heaped up wherever there was space. Over the years, Galena and the surrounding tri-state region of Kansas, Missouri, and Oklahoma, became dotted with these mounds, sometimes hundreds of feet high and covering several acres; the ground underneath was riddled with tunnels.

Mom did remark to me once that she remembered playing on top of the chat piles. *All the kids did after school. We climbed up and down and thought nothing of it.* No one knew or understood that the pilings were contaminated with poisonous lead and zinc dust, which they breathed in, or leeched into the groundwater below. The Environmental Protection Agency helped clean up the affected areas in 1983, but the old shafts and tunnels continued to give way, and still do. Picher, Oklahoma, just a mile across the border, was closed due to lead pollution, and Treece was eventually bought by the government, though a few families refused to leave the only home they had ever known.

Like the iron foundries and steel mills of Chicago where O. R. worked, the lead and zinc mines of southeast Kansas were just as dirty and dangerous for the men of Mom's family. Explosions and cave-ins were common. Charles Messer, Mom's maternal great-grandfather, died in 1915 of injuries sustained from an accident. "Messer was employed as a foreman and was working in a drift of the mine with George Bady and Roy Munson," noted his obituary, "when he was caught under several tons of dirt and rocks which fell from the roof. Although his injuries consisted of a crushed leg, internal injuries and body bruises, hope at first was expressed for his recovery."[5]

He was only 35, and left behind a widow and six children, the oldest of whom, Ada Mae, Mom's grandmother, was 15 years. I wondered how the family survived, but his obituary also noted that he was a member of A.O.U.W.—the Ancient Order of United Workers, an early fraternal organization that provided insurance for its members. Some widows and wives of disabled miners were forced to become the breadwinners in the family, sewing, taking in laundry, or selling sandwiches or fried chicken. A few of these cottage industries went on to become landmark restaurants in nearby Crawford County—Chicken Mary's and Chicken Annie's.

A month after her father's death, desperate, perhaps, to escape some of the burdens of helping her mother care for the family, Ada eloped with one Thomas Jefferson Timms, known mostly as Jefferson. He was only 18 and she was 15, but both lied about their ages on the marriage certificate stating they were 21 and 18. The feckless teens had not given a thought on how they were to live, so

Carol Winkler Kotsch

they moved in with Jefferson's domineering grandmother, who made life so unpleasant for Ada that she went back to her mother's home after only a few months. Jefferson refused to leave his grandmother and "spent his time in company with other women openly." With her mother's help, Ada had the marriage annulled in July, 1916.

Less than a year later, in April, 1917, she married Baccus Derfelt—unusual names seemed to run in Mom's family. Baccus was a Greek baby name, and referred to "Dionysus", the Greek god of wine. It seems an odd choice for his German-English family which had been living in the area since about 1875. But Baccus, or Bacchus is also an English surname which means "bakehouse," or "bakery." Perhaps this is where his uncommon first name came from, though I've not been able to find it elsewhere in his family.

His father, Charles, owned a meat market, and Baccus worked behind the counter grinding meat. About a month after his marriage to Ada, he caught his left hand in the revolving knives, and his middle finger was cut off at the first joint. After it healed, he may have been reluctant to resume butchering, for in the 1920 census, his occupation is "mill man for lead and zinc mine."

Baccus and Ada make an attractive couple in the small, torn photograph I have of them: he, tall and ruggedly handsome, she, dainty and demure. Their only child, Bessie Julia Belle, who went by Judy, was born in December, 1917. Ada, however, could not be happy at home with her new family—perhaps she also yearned to get away from a small, rough mining town.

She seized that chance in 1923, abandoning husband and daughter to live in Omaha, Nebraska with another man. Even after he returned to Kansas at the behest of his wife, who had him arrested, he and Ada continued to live together in nearby Baxter Springs, which was surely shocking for that time in a small community. Baccus tried again with Ada, and she returned to her own home, but left again after a month or two, this time to Oklahoma with her first husband, Jefferson Timms. Referring to Baccus, Ada sniffed dismissively that *he fainted at the sight of blood*, and *I can't be married to someone like that*. Baccus gave up and di-

The Farm on the Wall

vorced her in September, 1924. He remarried in 1925 to Maude Timms, the widow, ironically, of Jefferson's uncle Charles. Bessie, my grandmother, mostly lived with her father and stepmother.

It was a pattern Ada would follow throughout her life. She was married seven times to six different men, Mom told me once; she and Jefferson remarried shortly after her divorce from Baccus. In between husbands, she would live in shacks, and support herself waitressing at cafés. About 1928, she married a John Poole. The 1930 census shows them living in Corpus Christi, Texas, where he owned a grocery store. But in 1935, Ada was in Taft, California with a new husband, Jack Call, who was probably working in the oil fields. Newspaper clippings indicate a Mr. Rathbun somewhere in the picture, but I've not found any trace of him.

In 1940, she was back in Galena. She never did really make it out of a small town into a big city, dying at Coldwater, Kansas in 1965. We made a trip to Coldwater once to visit her and her current husband, Alonzo Richardson, bringing them some of our surplus kittens for their house. I was more interested in the red dirt I saw and didn't pay much attention to her.

Baccus continued working in the mines. By 1930, he was listed as a powder man in the mines, and was responsible for delivering the powder, dynamite, caps, detonators, fuses, and the like, to the miners. The drilling and dynamiting filled the mines with silica dust. The men in the mines were exposed to it the most, but the dust was everywhere in the town. Silicosis was a major industrial disease in the tri-state mining region, but the legislatures of Missouri, Oklahoma and Kansas never recognized it or tuberculosis as a compensable disease.[6] As Baccus—and thousands of other miners—inhaled the silica dust, the sharp-edged particles cut and scarred the tissue in his lungs, making it harder for him to breathe. His damaged lungs could no longer expand and contract as efficiently, decreasing the oxygen they could transmit, much like O. R. The longer men stayed in the mines, the worse they could expect it to become. "Workers who began work in their late teens or twenties could expect to contract silicosis by the time they were 40."[7] Baccus died of tuberculosis at 41, when Mom was

Carol Winkler Kotsch

two years old.

Some of the afflicted miners tried to repair their lungs by inhaling aluminum dust from a portable powder mill, a therapy used around 1944-49.[8] The powdered aluminum was packaged in small metal canisters of two and one half grams. Two miners at a time would breathe daily from the machine a few minutes at a time, until they reached 30 minutes, eventually completing 200 treatments. "There is no definite evidence that aluminum retarded the further development of silicosis."[9] The Jasper County Tuberculosis Hospital in nearby Webb City treated many of the miners.

Galena was a rough mining town with rough inhabitants, but slowly, churches and schools were built, sometimes on top of rich deposits, and began to civilize the coarse edges. By the 1890s, Galena had 265 producing mines, two banks, 36 grocers and more than four dozen other retail stores.[10] In 1910, the population was just over 6,000.[11] The area prospered for years, and Baxter Springs was "believed to be one of the wealthiest towns in Kansas and was reputed to have more millionaires per capita than any city in the U.S."[12]

After a few decades, however, the days of a "Poor Man's Camp" were gone, as the shallow deposits were worked out.[13] Heavy machinery and large crews were necessary to go after the deeper veins, and small-time operators now found themselves working as day laborers for big companies. When the 1935 National Labor Relations Act guaranteed private sector employees the right to organize into trade unions, bargain and strike, if need be, big mine owners didn't want any of it. Though union organizers prevailed, company officials refused to negotiate. The International Union of Mine, Mill, and Smelter Workers called a strike on May 8.

The mining companies retaliated by forming their own "company union", the Tri-State Metal Mine and Smelter Workers Union, more commonly called the "Blue Card Union", to replace them.[14] On June 28, the International Union fought back. "A crowd estimated at between 75 and 100 strikers laid siege on the Eagle-Picher smelter at Galena at 9 o'clock last night and began firing sporadically into the smelter office in which 12 special

The Farm on the Wall

guards were fortified behind desks and other office furniture." Strikers also blocked Route 66, throwing rocks and shooting at the Blue Card Union men. "Martial law to be invoked at Galena" read the headline on the June 29, 1935, edition of the Joplin Globe. Governor Landon called out three units of National Guard troops to help the "hopelessly outnumbered" deputy sheriffs restore order.[15]

The violence continued for a couple of years and finally died out. In the small mining museum in Galena, there is a group picture of the mining and smelting crew of Eagle-Picher dated June 15, 1936, that shows all the men with smiling faces; my grandpa, Jack Dugan, is on the front row, thinking, perhaps, of his wife and baby daughter, my mother. The mines stayed active until the '70s, until the ore was played out, and the town's population began to decline, and so did the area's economy.

Mom and her family were long gone by then. In 1942, when she was seven years old, Jack, her father, was drafted out of the mines and sent to Jefferson Barracks, Missouri, as a private in the Air Corps. He trained as a mechanic and was ultimately returned to Kansas and stationed at the newly created Army airfield in Dodge City where his family joined him. Mom's brother would be born there.

This airfield was part of the Army Air Forces 70,000 Pilot Training Program, jump-started on August 6, 1942, to provide more pilots for the war effort. With its wide-open spaces and sparse population, Kansas was an ideal training location. Completed in just 18 months, each of the 13 bases constructed for the war effort had at least three runways, several taxiways, and a large parking apron.[16] The Dodge City Army Airfield became one of three B-26 Marauder Training Bases, though there were also trainees for the Free French Air Force, as well as the Women's Air Force Service Pilots.[17] My grandfather would help keep the planes flying.

As the war began to draw to an end, the base closed almost as quickly as it had opened. In February 1945, the *Boot Hill Marauder* observed, "Pfc Jack Dugan has the right idea--ask him

Carol Winkler Kotsch

about his postwar plans."[18] The Dugan family stayed on in Dodge City, and Grandpa took a job as a mechanic at an automotive dealership, the Owens-Maser Motor Company, having no desire to return to the mines. He referred to those days only once that I can remember; when he learned that I liked to collect rocks, he gave me an almost perfect heavy cube of galena he had saved for some reason. *Found it while I was in the mines,* he casually remarked. *You can have it now.*

You were named after your grandmother, Jackie. She didn't say much when your father and I told her, but I could tell she was pleased. Her only comment was that she hoped we had not given you her middle name of Mae, which she disliked, and that Jacqueline was an awfully long name to learn to spell. She and her father were close, and I suspect she was named after him, but I never knew for certain.

10

Another Generation Begins

After Mom and Dad married in 1955, they moved into Auntie and Uncle's house up the hill. Dad also had a taste for rhubarb pie, and they transplanted some from Grandma's garden down the hill, next to the windmill up the hill, where Mom could easily pick some. I was born, girls, two years later in July, and my brother, your Uncle David, followed in August of the next year. I spent my first three years in Auntie and Uncle's old house, but have only the vaguest memory of riding a tricycle in a living room that was not the living room of the house I later knew and lived in.

There was also a barn on the hill, a horse and cattle barn with a hay mow built by Mr. Sweeney. I played in it occasionally whenever I walked up the hill, but it wasn't as interesting as the barn down the hill. Mr. Sweeney, however, used it for more than storing hay. Part of the floor was kept bare, and a piano was stored in a corner. It was known as quite a dance place, Dad said, and alcohol was served, a big attraction in dry Kansas.

Your grandparents hadn't been married very long when a man

stopped by the house on the hill and asked Dad if this was the old Sweeney place. He had gone to lots of dances in the barn he said, and wrecked his Model T there one night. A nice-looking young lady was present at one of the dances, and he was paying some attention to her, when another man approached the couple. Fearful that he was going to get beat up, he took off running for his car, put it in gear, and sped off without turning the carbide headlights on. He ran straight into the hog pen and tore out the front axle. It turned out the other man just wanted to offer him a shot of good whiskey.

After Uncle bought the property, he and Grandpa tore out the loft and put grain bins in to store the wheat harvest. It stored wheat and grain trucks for many years, but eventually the building became unstable and Dad tired of farming around it. It was torn down in 1974. An aerial crop sprayer later told Dad he missed the old barn, as he used it for a landmark when searching for the farms where he was hired to spray the corn and milo for pests.

Grandpa probably could have kept farming for several more years after Mom and Dad married, but technology was changing the way of farming he knew. He had started out with horses and learned to use tractors. The old one-way disk plow he and Uncle used after wheat harvest was now obsolete. The one-way, which consisted of a series of metal disks set at the same vertical angle, was invented by a farmer in nearby Meade County. It broke up the hard ground, and didn't turn all the wheat stubble into the ground, which provided some cover. But, when it was overused, the soil became pulverized and would blow easily.[1] Now, farmers were using sweeps instead, sharp V-shaped blades which slipped under the stubble and killed the weeds, but left more cover on the ground. Furthermore, farmers with water on their property were moving away from dry-land farming to using irrigation wells instead.

It was time to let his son handle it. Grandpa and Grandma retired in 1960. They planned to follow Auntie and Uncle to Dodge to live, and our family would then move into the larger house down the hill. But before they left, I somehow understood what

The Farm on the Wall

was going on, and walked down the hill by myself to see Grammie. The house was all topsy-turvy in preparation for the move, but I remember that she made me some pancakes.

Grandpa had loaded up most of the old and battered furniture that had served for so many years and headed to the dump. He and Grammie were anxious to buy new furnishings for their new house, after years of doing without. It was good furniture, though, under the scratches and dents, solid pieces Mom knew she could refinish as good as new. She caught Grandpa as he was pulling out of the driveway. *You don't want that old stuff,* he declared. *It's just old junk.*

He got rid of everything except one piece: an old wash stand that had made the trip from the home in Lockport. Grandpa was not a sentimental man—he couldn't afford to be—but the old wash stand must have had some memories associated with it. It didn't go inside the new Dodge City home, however, but was kept in the garage, where it held paint cans, motor oil, and garden tools. When it became stained and dirty, he gave it a fresh coat of paint. Grandpa knew Mom was keeping her eye on it, and after Grammie died, he gave it to her.

Mom set to work right away; she stripped off layer after layer after layer of old paint—seven colors, I think she counted—until she revealed the beautiful maple grain underneath. Patiently she sanded down all the scars and dents until it shone like satin, and then bought an antique wash basin and pitcher to put on top of it, just as it had once held when my grandpa was a boy. The only thing stored inside was a basket of the bows from our wedding gifts which you girls would pull out and play with when you were little.

Once they moved into their Dodge City home, they still kept to a farm schedule, rising early to eat breakfast by 6:30, dinner at 11:30, and supper at 5:30. Grandpa didn't quite know what to do with himself in retirement. Grandma kept busy with church and housework, but hard work was all Grandpa had ever known. He had a vegetable garden and grew tomatoes, and made trips to the grocery store for Grandma, and watched game shows on television. On Wednesdays, he went to the cattle sale at McKinley-Winter, and reported back to Dad how the market was doing. He visited with Uncle and took daily walks to monitor new homes going up, sometimes chatting with the construction crew. For a few years he was a census-taker—not the ten-year federal census, but the state census, Dad thought.

Not long after Mom and Dad's move down the hill, Auntie and Uncle's old house up the hill was sold and moved to the town of Satanta, about thirty miles to the west of Montezuma. For a time, Mom and Dad toyed with the idea of somehow turning the open basement into a swimming pool for me and my brother, but decided it would be too impractical and dangerous, and so it was filled in. I could still find the foundations of it, though, when I wandered around up the hill, and the little patch of rhubarb still came up each spring.

The last time I saw the old farmhouse at the bottom of the hill was during Christmas break of 1977. By then, Mom and Dad had moved into a new house halfway up the hill, a dream house they had been planning for some time. The sprawling 1,400 square foot ranch house was custom-built in Lubbock, Texas, and hauled up on the back roads to the farm. A "Dodge City" house, we would have called it when I was little. I had never lived in a house with central air and heat before. The furniture from the old house that Mom wanted to keep was already moved in. I unpacked my few items into my new bedroom, but it wasn't really mine; I'd be heading back to college in just a few weeks.

In the morning, Dad and I walked down to the old house. It looked small and shabby on the outside. Inside it was stripped bare, and it was if I noticed for the first time the cracks and stains and chips on the bare walls and floors. Even the floor seemed to sag. Silently, we walked around the empty, echoing rooms, and left.

The bones of the old house were still good, though, and Dad sold it for $5000. After I went back for another semester, it was jacked up off the foundations and hauled away. The basement was filled in and Dad enlarged the corrals over it for his cattle.

The Farm on the Wall

Only the trees were left to mark where the house had been, and even they died off.

But when I look at the old house in the picture hanging on the wall, I remember it the way it was when I was growing up. It was hot in the summer and cold in the winter, but I never noticed much, except in the winter, when the icy drafts in my bedroom sent me out to dress by the furnace grate set in the living room floor. It was the only warm spot in the house, except the kitchen.

My room was in the southwest corner, girls, just to the left of the door in the front porch that faces south. Two cedar trees are growing in front of it. It was a tiny little cube made even smaller by all my books and my rock collection. A maple tree grew outside the west window, and when the sun went down in the spring and summer, my room would be filled with green light, while leafy shadows swayed silently on the wall. At night, the moon would wake me and I would make my own shadows. From the living room, I could hear the clock given to O. R. and Mary in 1890 as a wedding present, chiming out the hours. Sometimes on those full-moon nights, I would throw a blanket over my shoulders to keep off the mosquitoes and creep out of the house to wander around. The dog knew he was not to bark as he followed me silently up and down the hill.

As I explored the house, I would find occasional reminders of my grandparents and great-grandparents. Down in the basement, forgotten by everyone else, were my grandmother's abandoned fruits and vegetables in the familiar Mason canning jars, lined up in neat rows on the dusty shelves of the corner cupboard, and changed by time into unidentifiable masses. Over in another corner of the basement, the names of my father and his brother were scratched in the crudely poured concrete ledge. I stumbled across a shoemaker's last and a sausage grinder that had been stored away years ago and wondered about a way of life only a couple of generations from mine.

You can just barely make it out in the picture, but there was a clothesline to the right of the windmill. Grandpa and Uncle made it from used pipes. Before Grandpa added a gas drier to the base-

Carol Winkler Kotsch

ment, Grammie hung her clothes downstairs during the winter on wire lines Grandpa had attached to the ceiling. Mom and Dad added an electric dryer on the back porch when they moved in, but continued to use the old gas washer in the basement, leftover from Grandma's time.

It did not have a spin cycle like you are used to today, so after the clothes were clean, they had to be fed by hand through the wringer. I loved helping push the heavy, dripping wet towels and jeans through the wringer and watching them come out damp and flat, but Mom had to watch me closely to make sure I didn't get my fingers caught in it. Then she loaded the clothes into the basket, carried them up the basement steps and outside to hang. I was too short to reach the lines, but handed clothespins up to Mom, and played inside the billowing rows of sheets and towels; at night I would fall asleep to the sweet freshness of sun-dried bedclothes.

There were two bookcases in the living room, one on either side of the door. Mom collected antique clocks which she displayed on the top shelves and hung on the wall above the cases. If I was extremely careful, I was permitted to wind them up with the clock key while she watched to make sure I didn't wind them too tightly. If one was slow, I would ever so gently nudge the hands so that they all chimed simultaneously.

The clock I loved the most was the one O. R. and Mary received as a wedding present in 1890, a shelf clock about eighteen inches tall that chimed the hour and half hour. The dark walnut case was outlined with curves and wings on the sides and top and bottom, and vines and flowers were press-molded across the front. "Gingerbread" clocks they were sometimes called, produced in great numbers in the late 1800s and sitting in the kitchens of lower and middle-class homes. On Saturday nights when Dad and his brother went to visit O. R. and Mary in Montezuma where they moved after they retired from the farm, Dad always looked forward to winding that clock himself and listening to it chime.

My second favorite clock came from the Graves family, Lura and Nellie's parents, who had followed their daughters after they married and moved west not far from our farm. After my Graves great-grandparents died, and the house was being cleaned out, Mom and Dad got to pick out something to remember them by—a round mantel clock with curved, sloping sides; it was as plain and simple as O. R.'s clock was ornate. But instead of simply striking the hour, it played a melody. At a quarter past, the first line chimed; the half hour repeated the first line and added a second; at a quarter to the hour, a third line. Finally, at the top of the hour, the entire four-part song played from start to finish, and then the hour tolled. When I opened the back and peeked inside, I could see tiny hammers striking the wires, pealing out the same tune I would hear from Big Ben when I travelled to London while in college. The "Westminster Quarters," it's called; I thought it was unique to our clock.

I ran in and out of the house dozens of times during the day, going in through the door you see on the east side. I tracked in dust during the summer, and snow and mud during the winter. The ground was littered with goat-head stickers and sandburs, but my brother and I preferred to go barefoot. Then Mom would have to dig broken-off thorns out of our leather-tough feet with one of her sewing needles. Sometimes the splinter was in so deep she couldn't get it out, and we would have to limp for a day or two while it festered and came to the surface.

Every time I ran in and out, I glanced up at the small metal pie-pan with tiny, pleated edges that hung close to the ceiling in one corner of the kitchen. It was painted the same color as the rest of the walls. I often wondered why my mother had hung a pie-pan on the wall, but never bothered to find out. Finally, on a hot, sleepy afternoon in July, when the cicadas were buzzing so loudly in the elm trees outside that I could hear them indoors, I looked up from the debris of the Sunday papers and asked my father why it was there.

That, he told me, was not a pie-pan, but a flue-cover, that it hid the hole left behind from the stovepipe of the old coal-burning stove. Though the house now boasted a gas furnace, once it had been heated by coal and had a chimney. There was a water tank on one end of the old stove, and every morning during the fall and winter, his father set the coals to burning, in order to heat the house and supply hot water. During the summer Grandma used a kerosene stove that wouldn't heat up the house as much. As soon as the house was warm enough, it was time for the rest of the family to get up.

An old-fashioned coal-burning stove sounded very like something from the fairy tales that I loved to read, but I had never noticed any coal around the house, or anywhere else on the farm, for that matter. *Where did you get the coal from*, I wanted to know? *Oh, it was shipped by train from Dodge*, Dad told me, *and sold by the hardware store in Montezuma. What they did was to let farmers back their trucks up to the boxcar and shovel out the coal they needed themselves. That way,* he added, *the hardware store didn't have the trouble of unloading it themselves and hauling the coal to the bin at the store.* Once home, Dad and his brother would shovel the coal down a chute to land in a dusty heap in the basement. Anyone who went downstairs was expected to fill up the coal scuttle if it happened to be empty.

Then Dad pointed to the now-empty corner and told me that was where he used to sit in the wintertime, with his feet propped up against the door of the stove so he could stay warm while he ate his ice cream. Winter was the only time he got to eat ice cream, he said, since his family didn't have a refrigerator to store it in, let alone the money to buy such a treat. Anyway, there wasn't electricity on the farm yet. Incredulous and wide-eyed at this lack of essentials, I demanded to know how he got his ice cream.

Some of the ingredients were already on the farm, I found out. Grandma whisked fresh cream and eggs provided by the milk cows and chickens, added a few drops of vanilla and some sugar purchased from town, and cooked everything gently on the coal range in the kitchen. She had to stir it constantly, making sure that it did not come to a boil. When it was thick enough to coat a spoon, she poured the mixture into a bowl and cooled it on the countertop.

The Farm on the Wall

In the meantime, Grandpa, Dad, and Uncle Lowell went outside to the corral, carrying an ax and a gunnysack. They cut a hole through the ice in the stock tank so the cattle could drink and saved the chunks of ice in the sack. Back inside the house, they crushed the ice into smaller pieces, and got out the rock salt and the ice cream churn.

Grandma poured the cooled mixture of eggs and cream and sugar into a metal canister, put in the paddle, and secured the lid. Next, she fitted on the crank, a handle that rotated the paddle around and around. Grandpa lowered the canister into a wooden bucket and began to pack layers of salt and ice around the canister until it reached the top. As the ice began to melt from the salt, the freezing temperature was lowered, and the contents of the canister began to get colder.

Now it was Dad's turn to help. As he turned the crank, the paddle churned the contents, keeping it from freezing solid, and mixed in air so it would be soft and light. As it got colder and colder, it also became thicker, and it was harder to crank. When Dad's arm was ready to drop off, Uncle Lowell took over. After about thirty minutes, it was so thick that he could no longer turn the crank, and it was time to stop.

Grandpa lifted the canister out of the wooden bucket, and placed it in the sink, but the ice cream was not ready to eat. It had to ripen for a few minutes, Grandma told them, and it would taste better if they waited. Dad and his brother fidgeted impatiently until finally Grandma scooped out ice cream into bowls for everyone. The two brothers positioned their chairs in front of the stove, opened the door and propped their feet just inches from the hot coals as they hastily spooned up their special winter treat, shivering all the while.

I listened in open-mouthed amazement and Dad laughed at the expression on my face. *Yes,* he said, *we did have an icebox, but we could only afford to buy ice at harvest time, and that was saved for the thirsty harvest crew. The rest of the time Grandma kept the butter and groceries in the pantry—right here behind you,* he said, pointing to the narrow dark room just behind the kitchen—*and the butter would get so soft it would run like oil.*

Ice was imported from Dodge City by A. P. Bargar, the local grocer, and sold a block at a time out of his garage. In 1934, this enterprising small-town businessman developed a plan to convert a railroad refrigerator boxcar into an ice-making plant but lacked the funds to purchase some Freon. He approached the bank for a $10 loan, but the banker, Ellis McReynolds, turned him down, claiming he would likely blow up the town. Somehow neighbor and entrepreneur Henry X. Smith learned of A. P.'s proposal and reached into his own pocket for the money. The cost of a block of ice dropped down to a quarter, and the Winkler family began to make a habit of stopping by the grocery store after church on summer Sundays to pick up a block.

The old black '35 V/8 Ford was crammed full of Grandma and Grandpa and Auntie and Uncle and all the cousins, so the ice was lashed to the front bumper and covered in a burlap sack kept in the car for just such a purpose. Grandpa drove home the seven miles from town to the farm as fast as he could. Grandma filled the canister of the ice cream maker with the cream and egg mixture and placed it in a wood tub. The men crushed the ice, packed it around the canister, sprinkled some gray rock salt on top, and set the children to work churning. Some thirty minutes later it was ready, and now Dad could enjoy his treat in the middle of the summer, but he never forgot the taste of homemade ice cream eaten in the winter next to the old coal-burning stove.

In 1938, Grandpa and Uncle had a fairly good wheat and milo crop, Uncle Lowell remembered, enough that they installed a butane gas tank, which made it possible to put in a butane stove and refrigerator. Grandma began freezing ice cream inside this new convenience instead. The days of hand cranking were over. The next time I went outside, I scratched in the dirt outside the basement window and unearthed several small, crumbly chunks of coal.

11

Kitchen Table

Like any good farmhouse, the kitchen was the center of almost all of our activities—homework, first aid, experiments—but fixing meals, of course, prevailed. Cooking for my hard-working father and hired man was a never-ending chore, and as soon as one meal was finished and the kitchen cleaned up, we had to start preparing for the next one. When I look back and see my mother in the house, she was usually standing at the old gas stove stirring something in the pan, or bending over the stained and pockmarked porcelain sink, cleaning up.

In the cool of a summer morning, Mom would send me out to pick tomatoes and green beans and cucumbers and dig up potatoes and pull onions from the garden behind the supply tank. Then with the meat from one of Dad's calves that had been hand-fed with grain, or a chicken from the flock, we could boast that our entire meal was produced from the farm. We sometimes quibbled about dessert but decided we could still count the flour used to make it, even if there was no way of knowing whether it came

Carol Winkler Kotsch

from our farm or not.

    I had always thought Mom was a good cook, so I was surprised when she admitted to me many years ago that she never liked it. But cook she had to do as a farmwife, three times a day, seven days a week. There were some convenience foods available, but most of our meals were made from scratch. At least she didn't have to go out and kill and clean two chickens in the morning for dinner like my grandmother did. Growing up on the farm, we ate heavier meals than you girls would be used to—it was mostly meat and potatoes—but we also engaged in more physical activity. I became used to cooking big meals for hungry, hardworking men, and when your father and I were first married, I had to learn to scale back the amount I made.

    For breakfast, it was bacon and eggs and toast or frozen honeybuns—a big treat—or pancakes and syrup. We ate cereal too, and I put away my share of sugary goodness, as I was not a big fried egg eater. Pancakes were my favorite, made from Bisquick. I grew up eating oatmeal cooked on the stove as microwaves were a long way off. When your grandpa was growing up, his father would sometimes bring in a few handfuls of wheat at night to soak until morning. Grandma would boil it on the stove, and they would eat that for breakfast, with a little sugar sprinkled in.

    The noon meal was always dinner, never lunch. It was the heaviest meal of the day. We would have meatloaf and scalloped potatoes, fried chicken and mashed potatoes with gravy, roast beef with potatoes and carrots and onions, macaroni and cheese, round steak, T-bone steak, biscuits and dried beef gravy, and tuna and noodles. A big favorite was a pot of diced potatoes covered with cheese sauce to go with whatever meat Mom was serving. Very occasionally we might have fried fish, which Mom persisted in making from time to time, despite the fishy smell that lingered and the negative comments from my brother and me. I used lots of lemon juice to make it go down easier.

    Aside from spaghetti and meatballs, we didn't eat any other kinds of ethnic foods until the recipes filtered out to southwest Kansas. At that time, spaghetti was an unknown novelty to our family, and one Mom saved for a company meal. Later, when the newness wore off, we had it frequently, though it and macaroni and cheese were the only kinds of pasta dishes I was aware of. I remember when she made Oriental Casserole, which featured then exotic Chinese vegetables like bean sprouts and water chestnuts mixed in with the ever-present cream of mushroom soup and browned hamburger.

I ate about everything Mom made, but I drew the line at liver, and there was always a battle when it was served, as I was the only one who refused to eat it. My father declared I could leave the table hungry, which I did. I was very fond of tongue, however, though we didn't have it nearly as often as I would have liked. To me, it was better than roast beef, tender and full of flavor. It was my brother who made a fuss about eating it, until one day Mom served it cut into bite-sized pieces and called it roast beef. He ate it in blissful ignorance and could not be convinced that it was indeed tongue.

Mom also served some kind of gelatin salad at nearly every meal, which I would pass around without helping myself. Oddly for most farm families, we never had bread at the meal, and Mom very seldom made any fresh bread herself; our bread was limited to the soft, tasteless, limp white loaves from the store, which was all we knew. I tried making bread from time to time after I married, but the results were not always edible. It wasn't until I started my own family that I tried again with an award-winning recipe from Viola Unruh, a bread-baking neighbor, and found success.

There were vegetables, cooked until they were limp and gray-green, as was typical of the day, mostly peas, green beans and broccoli. Mom's green beans were really good though, if she took fresh ones from the garden and cooked them on the stove with a bit of bacon on top. The dog got the leftover bacon. In the summer we loved corn on the cob, but Mom said she always thought of corn as fattening pigs for market. When I learned to cook Chinese style, she leaned over and whispered to me that the vegetables were still crisp and that I ought to cook them a bit longer next time.

Carol Winkler Kotsch

And after the meal—dessert. We had pies, mostly fruit, though Mom would sometimes make a lemon meringue. I loved pie, and rhubarb and boysenberry were my favorites. The rhubarb came straight from the patch planted by my grandparents. We also made peach and apple and cherry pies, frequently from scratch, but sometimes we were in a hurry, and used canned pie filling instead. It always felt a little bit like cheating.

Light and flaky, Mom's crust could not be bettered, and it was one of the very first things she taught me to make. Two cups flour, one cup of shortening and a half cup of ice water for a two-crust pie and divide in half for a one-crust pie. First, she showed me how to use a fork and cut in the shortening and flour until I had pea-sized particles. Next, some water that had been chilled with ice cubes, since that made the dough easier to handle, but only a little water at a time, until the dough would hold together. She slipped a cover over the rolling pin so the dough wouldn't stick, and got out the pastry cloth, sprinkled some flour in the middle and showed me how to roll the dough out into a circle, being careful not to work it too much or it would be tough.

Then she folded the circle in half, placed it in the pie pan and unfolded it. The sliced apples, which had already been mixed with sugar and flour, went in next, and we rolled out another crust to cover the top. Other times we slipped in cherries, or boysenberries, another favorite of mine. She fluted the edges with her fingers and thumb, took the knife and cut the initial of the fruit on top so it wouldn't bubble over, and we were done. Any leftover dough was rolled out again, placed in another pie pan and sprinkled with sugar and cinnamon and baked for my brother and me to eat. In later years, she started making her pie crusts out of lard instead of shortening and added a teaspoon of vinegar. They were extraordinarily flaky, but I still preferred the recipe I grew up with.

We had cakes, too; I loved the apple nut cake she made, but that was usually for holidays. The chocolate sheet cake was always a staple. Coffee cakes, I think, and I remember a banana spice cake, too. Mom made a no-bake cherry cheesecake that she and Dad especially enjoyed, but I did not care for cream cheese—or thought I didn't as I refused to try it—and so it took longer to disappear from the refrigerator.

Cookies fell under my jurisdiction. I made dozens and dozens and dozens during the summer, mostly during harvest. Sugar cookies, peanut butter, chocolate chip, oatmeal, snicker doodles, molasses—I filled up the kitchen counter with cookies. One year Beefy's wife, Gennie, gave me a recipe that Mary Winkler had given to her for raisin nut cookies. It was written on heavy paper, and was brown and brittle to the touch, but I could still read my great-grandmother's handwriting. The top had crumbled away, so I didn't know what she called them. I made them as well and laminated the recipe in order to preserve it.

Once the cookies had cooled, sometimes Mom would pack them up in a Tupperware container, along with a fresh jug of iced tea, and let me drive the car to the field where the men were cutting. I always jumped at the chance to drive by myself. One day I decided that orange-flavored Tang would be a welcome change, but quickly discovered that the men felt differently. The next day I made sure to fill the jug with tea.

Supper was a lighter meal. Sometimes it was just fried potatoes and cottage cheese, or grilled cheese sandwiches, scrambled egg sandwiches, or maybe leftover roast beef sandwiches. During harvest, Mom would cook roast or ham and then grind up the meat and add diced pickles, onion, mustard and mayonnaise. In the winter we ate lots of soup—chicken noodle, ham and bean, beef and vegetable, and beef stew. Mom put them together in the afternoon and they simmered away until Dad came in from feeding and checking the cattle, his hands and face purple and swollen from the cold.

Mom taught me how to make pie crusts and cut up a chicken, and Grammie taught me to put a tablespoon of vinegar into fresh milk if there was no buttermilk for the recipe, but most of my cooking skills I learned through trial and error and cookbook directions. One year for Christmas I received an Easy-Bake Oven and was thrilled with the miniature pans and cake mixes. I re-

Carol Winkler Kotsch

member making a cake and frosting it and presenting it to Dad to eat.

When I was in the fourth grade, Pat Robertson, a classmate of Mom's from Dodge City, and now living straight south of us, gave me the *Betty Crocker Cookbook for Boys and Girls*. Betty was very careful and organized with us young cooks, breaking down the recipes step by step, and encouraging us to have everything laid out before we started. I learned to make chili and tuna burgers and cut radishes into roses. Pictures of her taste testers were in the front of the book; I crossed out the picture of Elizabeth because she wore braids like the Mennonite girls who sometimes teased me at school. I kept it all through high school and college and took it with me when I married; the back cover is missing now, and the pages are stained and loose.

I was permitted to make anything I found in Mom's cookbooks. The arrangement was that she would buy the ingredients and I would cook, but I had to clean up the mess I made, something I sometimes conveniently forgot to do. I remember making caramels and marshmallows with mixed results, but they were quickly eaten by the men nonetheless. One year we raised ducks, and when we butchered them, it seemed like the perfect time to try the duck à l'orange I found in a more sophisticated cookbook, but we discovered our tastes were not so continental. I don't remember what we did with the rest of the ducks, but I never had the urge to try duck à l'orange again.

When the dishes were washed and dried, and it wasn't quite time to start supper, I would find Mom huddled over the sewing machine that was squeezed into the kitchen. The ironing board was almost a permanent fixture next to it, and when it was taken down to make room for Mom's bridge club ladies, the kitchen seemed bare and empty. In the morning the mail was dumped on it and after school it held our books and jackets. Sometimes she was just patching the worn-out knees of jeans, or repairing a shirt torn while working on a tractor, but even these mundane sewing chores were done with the same careful attention for detail that she used to create the suits and dresses that were mistaken for store-bought.

The bridge club ladies always exclaimed over the outfits she created for me, but it took several years before I learned to appreciate her unerring sense of style. I disdained frilly dresses, preferring instead jeans and shorts and tee shirts. In the meantime, I had to endure trips to the fabric section at the old Eckles Department store in Dodge. Along with the First National Bank, the three-story building dominated downtown Dodge and our family hardly ever shopped anywhere else. The clothing at the Sears store did not live up to Mom's standards and I didn't set foot in one until after I was married.

As you stepped inside Eckles, leather goods, billfolds and purses and belts were on the right. Umbrellas were displayed as well, but we never had much use for one. Men's clothing was on the left, an uninteresting area I ignored. In between were the circular display tables, heavy round wooden counters with graduated shelves that looked like wooden wedding cakes frosted with shirts and ties. At Christmas time they held baskets of cheeses, sausage and jam. Then came the jewelry cases, which were more interesting to me. I lingered there as Mom walked on, to see if there were any gems I could recognize from my rock books.

Finally, in the back, was the fabric department. Mom sat down on one of the soda fountain stools in front of a table that was tilted at an angle so the heavy, awkward pattern books could be more easily viewed. Until I was older and could wander through the store on my own, there was little to do except spin around on the stool, which I could only do a few times until my annoyed mother made me stop, or get up and run my fingers along the rows of rainbow-colored spools of thread. She ignored my protests over the prissy-looking pattern she selected and calmly began selecting material.

The patient clerk, who knew my mother well, complimented her on the choice of fabric and remarked how cute I would look when it was finished, which I knew was not true, but could not say anything. The clerk dropped the bolt of material into the foot-deep channel that ran the length of the wooden cutting table. Then she tugged hard on the edge of the fabric, making the bolt flop over and over, until she had unwound enough. Next, she measured out the required amount, and swiftly and precisely cut it off. This waist-high groove was just the perfect size for me to slide from one end of the table to the other like a torpedo, but I had to do it when the clerk was helping Mom choose a zipper and thread to match and no one was paying attention to me.

Once I was older, then I could backtrack through the shoe department, and walk down the creaky stairs to the toy department in the basement, which it shared with house wares. Before I could get to the Hardy Boys, I had to walk past mixing bowls and kitchen utensils. Then came Barbie and her cousins, useless things to me, though the troll dolls were mildly appealing. I ignored the trucks and model cars, studied the games, and looked at microscopes and telescopes and wished them for my own. Then at last I came to the Hardy Boys and Nancy Drew and made a list of the titles I wanted for next Christmas and birthday.

An electronics department was located just off of fabrics. Washers and driers were on one side, and TVs and radios on the other. It was there that we saw our first color TVs, huge floor models, an unimaginable luxury at the time, though the color wasn't very good. If my brother had been dragged along with us, he would park himself in front of one, and my mother could continue shopping knowing he would not budge.

We ourselves had a small black and white television, a red one with a 12-inch screen that sat on top of a coffee table. The three channels we were able to get didn't offer much children's programming, but I watched Captain Kangaroo in the morning and John Gnagy's drawing show in the afternoon. Major Astro featured Superman reruns for years, and we pinned towels to our shoulders to serve as capes as we ran and leaped off the front porch with our arms outstretched. We knew better than to jump off the roof of the house while pretending to fly; the Major had warned us about some other children who had tried just that and gotten seriously hurt. Eventually we purchased a floor model ourselves, but it was still in black and white. We had to wait a few more years to afford a color set.

The Farm on the Wall

If we didn't need any shoes, the next stop was the mezzanine. The spiral staircase was narrow and steep and reminded me of a secret passageway. When other shoppers came down we had to squeeze to the side so we could pass each other. Eckles had installed an elevator for its customers, but you had to be sixteen to ride by yourself.

The mezzanine level curved in a half circle above the main floor. To our right were knick-knacks and small sculptures nestled around the needlework supplies. Mom liked to knit and crochet, and spent the winter stitching at needlepoint canvasses, which she later stretched and framed; after several years, they took up an entire wall. While she picked out some yarn, I would lean over the edge of the mezzanine railing and peer at the shoppers below.

Boys' clothing was at the end of the right-hand curve, another uninteresting area. If we were shopping there with my brother, I would distract myself with looking at the mural on the wall behind the Boy Scout supplies. Two scouts, dressed in neat uniforms, paddled a canoe down a clear, swift-flowing tree-lined river. It didn't look a thing like the shallow Arkansas that flowed lazily through Dodge. If Colorado was hoarding water in the John Martin Reservoir, then it would become just a trickle.

The left-hand curve of the mezzanine featured fine crystal and china and silverware. There the staircase continued, but now it opened up like a wide boulevard and took us majestically to the ladies' department on the second floor. The atmosphere changed as soon as we reached the top and stepped onto the plush carpet. The noise and clatter of the other departments faded away into a reverent hush as determined-looking ladies concentrated on selecting dresses. Even the lighting glowed differently.

Now I had to wait as Mom tried on dress after dress, growing more and more impatient and bored. She would study each one thoughtfully in the three-way mirror, and then go on to the next suit, or worse, try on one she had previously rejected. To pass the time, I posed in front of the three-way mirror myself, examining the back of my head, or hid among the racks of dresses. Once I painstakingly removed all the perforated price tags from a rack of suits in order to help the clerks. On the way home, I rolled down the window and tossed them out over the river.

If she had bought a new dress pattern for me that day, we were done, and I would be reprieved from trying anything on from the young misses' area. Otherwise I would have to go to the racks and choose something, which I did as uncooperatively as possible. Soon Mom's jaw clenched as I rejected one dress after another for being scratchy or tight or the wrong color. Eventually I would run out of excuses and she would choose for me, despite my anguished complaints.

It all changed in a few years as I grew into junior high and high school. Now I would hurry over to the junior department of my own accord and beg for something new to wear to school. It had to be short enough, though, for the mini-skirt trend. Mom watched patiently as I tried on outfit after outfit, holding her tongue at my new attitude, and reminding me that she could take up the hem at home. I wanted my skirts shorter than she would take them up, and she had to remind me that she could always shorten it, but if it was too short, she couldn't make it longer. In the end, I had to accept a compromise on the hem length, but I found I could roll up the waistband of my skirt before going to school and make it shorter that way.

Mom also shook her head over the skintight hip-hugging flared jeans that I loved to wear. *Clothes should drape the body and not encase it*, she gently reminded me. Her words fell on deaf ears at first, but later I recalled them and eventually found my own sense of style that would not have clashed with her own classic look.

Finally, we were finished, to my great relief. At the counter, the clerk made out a ticket for our purchases and Mom wrote out a check. The ticket and check were rolled up and slipped inside a small, metal canister which was whisked away in one of the pneumatic tubes that lined the store to the unseen accounting department. In a few minutes it returned with a hiss and a bump and the clerk handed over the receipt.

Once home, Mom carefully positioned the material and pattern on the kitchen table, making sure any stripes or patterns would match when sewn together. The snip-snip-snip-snip of her scissors as she cut out the pieces of my new outfit was nearly as regular and precise as the antique clocks ticking away in the living room. I fussed loudly as she tried the pinned-together pieces on me for size and complained as each pin pricked my arms and legs. She could not bear a loose thread or a crooked seam, and the insides of all her creations were as flawless as the outsides. The hum and click of the sewing machine filled the house on summer afternoons. As I grew older, she turned to making me classic wool skirts and jackets that still look very much in style even after 40 years.

When I became engaged to your father, she used her skills to produce an exquisite wedding dress for me. I selected the pattern and material this time and stood uncomplainingly still for as long as she required, ignoring the pins. She had sewn her own wedding dress but seemed indifferent to keeping it. I found it in the basement when I was little, and tried it on, dragging it all over the rough and dirty basement floor. Eventually, she tossed it out. I wanted to preserve her hard work on my dress, and had the delicate lace and fabric carefully cleaned and boxed away, to hold in trust for you girls. But wedding dresses are individual, and my mother would have been the first to recognize that what looked good on one generation might not suit another. Perhaps, if it survives, it will appeal to another descendant.

12

The Four Seasons of Growing Wheat

The life I knew on the farm moved in rhythm around the planting and harvesting of crops and feeding livestock for market. Wheat had been the draw for O.R. and my grandfather and uncle, but my grandpa started adding other crops and cattle in order to diversify. I grew up watching the wheat harvest, but also milo and to an increasing degree over the years, corn. Dad even dabbled in soybeans once or twice, and added hogs while I was in high school. Still, it was wheat that remained the most important cash crop, and each season had a part in its production.

After my birthday in late July, the summer was more than halfway over and there was nothing to look forward to except counting the days until the start of school. When I saw the yellow school bus on the horizon practicing running the routes in late August, then summer really was over, and it was time for fall. At school, I colored pictures of leaves red and orange and yellow, but autumn was more subdued in southwest Kansas. Our two lone maple trees turned yellow for a brief time, but the elms just became a dull brownish green. The buffalo grass was already brown and dry from the summer heat. Even the tough weeds in the ditches, the only green growing things aside from the crops, were withering. Soon they would produce a crop of their own: a host of tumbleweeds that would roll across the roads and fields and weigh down fences.

I had my own signs of fall that I looked forward to. The milo heads were turning color, from the bright yellow-green of early summer, to a rich, deep orange-red. Before long Dad would get out the combine from the long shed where it had sat since wheat harvest was over, and milo harvest would begin. But the real sign of fall for me was the day Dad would drill winter wheat. If it had been dry, he worried about enough moisture to sprout the seeds, and sometimes he would delay planting as long as possible in order to catch a late shower.

Once the wheat was planted, there was an impatient wait over the next week and a half to see if it was going to shoot up. Dad scanned the fields every day, and so did we, in serious imitation. And then one morning, while riding to school on the bus, with the late-rising autumn sun lighting up the fields, we could just make out the needle-thin spears coming up, a faint green haze against the rich brown furrows. It would grow about ankle-high during the rest of fall, and then Black Angus and red Hereford cattle would be pastured on it for a time. Unharmed by the grazing heifers, the wheat would lie dormant all winter, and then shoot up again in the spring, and I would play in it once more.

It quickly grew higher than my waist and headed out. Once that happened, we watched anxiously for storms that would damage the developing kernels. All too soon, the summer heat set in. In late May or early June, depending on how wet the spring had been, the wheat began to turn from green to gold. That was the signal for Dad to head over to the long shed and begin attaching the header to the combine. He and the hired man inspected it from top to bottom, checking belts and greasing chains, and starting it up to see if the engine needed work. Every other day, Dad stripped the kernels from a head and squeezed one with his thumbnail. If it was soft and milky, it was still too green. Finally, when the heads bent over, and the kernels were hard, Dad would make a test cut and haul it to the elevator in Cope-

The Farm on the Wall

land.

Outside all the local elevators, grain trucks lined up with test loads as all the farmers were waiting to see if their wheat was dry enough to cut. If the moisture tested higher than thirteen percent, the elevator would take it, but they would dock the price as it wouldn't store as well and had to be moved it from bin to bin and blended with dry wheat. A good year meant the wheat would weigh about sixty pounds per bushel. Less than that—fifty-five pounds and below—and the farmer would be docked in price.

If the wheat was too wet, then the combine sat in the farmyard while we waited for the wheat to dry out some more, and trusted that summer storms would hold off until after harvest. The ripe wheat could survive a storm, but then the quality of the grain would start to deteriorate, and the combine and trucks would bog down in the wet fields.

The very instant it was dry enough, Dad began to cut and everything else stopped for harvest. Every prudent farmer cut as soon as the wheat was ready. Once, a neighbor decided that his field could wait another day or two while he made a jaunt to Dodge City. A hailstorm hit that day and took out part of his crops.

During the frantic days of cutting wheat, it seemed that Mom would spend most of the morning making dinner to take to the field. Fried chicken and potato salad, or hamburgers and potato chips and baked beans, or ham and scalloped potatoes, it was all carefully packed into the trunk of the car, along with the jug of iced tea and the card table and chairs. When I was about nine or ten years old, she spread out the pastry cloth that was saturated with flour spilled from the creation of hundreds of desserts and taught me how to roll out dough for pie crust in that kitchen. It became my job to keep the men supplied with pies and cookies and cakes during harvest.

Sometimes the days were so still that the dust hung in the air long after we had gone by on our way to the field where Dad was cutting that day, and then it drifted slowly down to coat the sunflowers and dull their bright yellow petals. We parked the car at the edge of the field and began to set up the table and chairs in the shade of the grain truck as we waited for the combine to finish a round. When the bin on the combine was full, Dad would lower the spout and the wheat would spill into the grain truck in a whooshing rush of gold, with the chaff floating away. The hired man, having finished his meal, hopped up into the cab to head the combine down another row of uncut wheat, and it was Dad's turn to eat. We hardly saw him during harvest, as he was gone before the sun was up, and stayed out cutting until the grain elevator closed around midnight or later.

Sitting in the shade of the truck was not much cooler than standing in the sun, and eating in the field had long lost its novelty, so my brother and I would finish the meal even more quickly than Dad, who was ever anxious to get back to cutting while the weather held. We clambered up the truck to scoop out a handful of wheat, picked out the delicate green inchworms and the dirt and pebbles, and chewed and chewed the nutty kernels until we could blow a small, starchy bubble. We longed to hop over the side and play in the wheat, but this was strictly forbidden, as Dad and Mom were fearful that we would sink in over our heads and smother.

The hired hand pulled the tarp over the grain so it would not blow out of the truck, started up the engine, and lumbered off to unload the wheat at the elevator in Copeland, the flattest part of Gray County. We could easily see the 125-feet-tall grain elevator over 11 miles away.

Grain elevators dotted southwest Kansas like checker pieces on a gigantic board. "Green alligators," you girls called them when you were little. They dominated each small town, towering over the other buildings on each main street: a post office, a grade school and high school, a grocery store, a café, a hardware store and assorted implement dealers. Montezuma's prosperity showed with two grocery stores when I was growing up, plus a drugstore and a medical clinic, though it was hard to keep it staffed with a doctor.

When the meal was over, Mom packed up the remains of dinner and folded the table and chairs and stowed it all back into the

The Farm on the Wall

trunk of the car. My brother and I sprawled in the back seat, hot and tired and cranky, scratching at the red gouges on our legs made by the sharp-edged wheat stubble. On the way home, we added another layer of dust to the sunflowers. The dishes were unpacked and washed, the kitchen cleaned up, and then it was time to start planning supper.

Trips to Dodge or into town were cancelled during harvest, unless we needed to pick up a part from the implement dealer, and then we didn't have time to sit at the drugstore or shop, but had to hurry home so Dad could get the combine going again. We were confined to the house and kitchen and the farmyard; I could not saddle up for a ride as Mom worried a speeding grain truck might spook the horse.

Like all farm boys, my brother began driving the big grain trucks and the combine as soon as he was old enough, and in a pinch, Mom did too, but I only learned how to shift gears on the pickup. I expect other farmers' daughters of my generation would find that strange. I had frequent colds when I was little, though I don't remember them, but it was bad enough, apparently, that I had my tonsils removed in the second grade. It didn't help. I came down with pneumonia the next year and missed two weeks of school. Dad picked up my homework every day, and Mom helped me study after supper. My classmates sent me get-well cards and Valentines.

I spent my days resting on the couch, protesting that I didn't feel bad at all, and couldn't I please, please go outside. Marilyn Love, our neighbor to the west, brought over a large box; inside were seven smaller boxes with instructions to open one each day. I can't remember all she brought for me, but Marilyn knew I loved to read and included the book *The Little Lame Prince*. I kept it for many years. When I was well enough to go back to school, I had to stay inside at recess for a week or two; you can see the dark circles under my eyes in my school picture for that year.

A year or two later, the doctor diagnosed hay fever. There were no over-the-counter remedies then, but I was given a prescription to help, and told to stay out of the barn, and other places that might make me sneeze and cough. You might just as well have told the wind to stop blowing, but Dad never had me drive the grain truck.

In ten or twelve days, the rush of cooking and driving and cleaning would be over. The header was removed from the combine and stored away for the milo and corn harvest in the fall. Now the rhythm of farm work changed to checking irrigation wells that watered the growing corn and milo and plowing the wheat stubble under. Dad would again appear in the house to eat dinner and supper with us at the table.

It was too hot for wandering around now, and we spent most of our afternoons swimming and splashing in the stock tank. Dad rolled one out as soon as school was dismissed, right next to the supply tank by the windmill. We cleaned it out, screwed in the plug, and stuck in the hose. Then we had to wait for it to fill with water, a process that took several hours, since there was no pressure from the water supply tank. To help us endure the wait, we made a trip to town during the week and sipped Cokes at the drugstore. Mom sat in one of the booths up front, while I crept to the back where the comic books were kept and leafed through the latest adventures of Superman and Batman and Spiderman. Periodically one of the high-school student employees would be instructed to shoo me away or encourage me to buy one.

When Mom finished catching up on the news and gossip in town, it was time to leave. By the time we got back, the tank was full, and my brother and I jumped and splashed and paddled all afternoon in the luke-warm water, finally shedding wet swimsuits and towels in a soggy heap on the back porch when our toes and fingers became covered with deep wrinkles.

In a few days, green scum began to grow, and sleek, black water beetles somehow found their way into the tank. We chased after them underwater, pretending we were swimming through ocean seaweed. When it became too murky to see, we drained the water, tipped the tank over on its side to scrape it clean, and refilled it. It served us well for several years, but eventually we outgrew it. Then we turned it into a habitat for box turtles that lived

The Farm on the Wall

on an island of sand and rocks, while tadpoles bobbled in the warm shallows.

Sometimes when he was caught up with plowing wheat stubble, Dad would announce we'd be going on a picnic. Instead of getting us dressed and ready for church, Mom would spend the morning frying up chicken, while Dad checked the wells and picked up the Sunday paper in town. Then Mom packed the chicken in the car trunk, along with the potato salad and chocolate cake she'd made the night before and added a jug of lemonade and a watermelon. My brother and I scurried around to find towels and swimsuits and shoes, and we'd be off. I made sure I packed a book to read in the back seat while we drove.

Usually we went to Wright Park in Dodge City, which I liked well enough. There were tall shady trees and thick green grass, very unlike the farm. I played on the swings, climbed the monkey bars, and explored the old bandstand. There was a small zoo, but it was old and cramped, and I did not like watching the tired-looking animals standing on the bare cement. After we finished eating, Dad would come with us down to the Arkansas River where we tried to catch minnows and crawdads while Mom read the paper under the shade.

Or we might drive to Finnup Park in Garden City, which had a more elaborate zoo and playground area, and the world's largest, free, concrete municipal swimming pool. Grandpa and I took you girls there once; do you remember? Occasionally, we drove to Meade Lake or Clark County Lake, where I marveled at the red soil and picked up selenite crystals to add to my rock collection. But my favorite place to go was Scott County Lake, though it was an hour and a half drive. The last ten or so miles took us across bare, empty space, even more bare and empty than I was used to, and then, unexpectedly, a green valley with a shimmering lake and craggy white bluffs opened up right before us. I was fascinated by the spring that fed the 100-acre lake and could not get enough of watching the clear water bubbling up right out of the ground. It was hard to believe that I was seeing water that wasn't coming from a windmill or irrigation well.

We looked at the ruins of El Quartelejo, a pueblo built by Taos Indians who had revolted from the Spanish in New Mexico and fled to the northeast looking for shelter, read about the Battle of Beaver Creek, where the U.S. Cavalry was beaten back by a band of Cheyenne escaping from an Oklahoma reservation in 1878, and toured the Steele home, built of native sandstone by early settlers in 1908.

We found a good picnic table right up next to the lake and my brother and I waded and splashed in the water, while Mom set out the food. I found fresh-water clam shells with bands of green and brown on the outside, and iridescent mother of pearl on the inside. I cleaned up the prettiest to take home.

After our picnic lunch had settled, Dad and I hiked along some of the trails and I found some fossil clams, ancestors, no doubt, of the ones I had just found in the lake. Once again, I picked up the best to take home and add to my collection. Then it was time for the long drive home. We were tired and sunburned and sticky. The car was unpacked, swimsuits tossed in the corner, and rocks and fossils added to my collection. Dad headed out to check the wells again, and the next day was back to the unvarying routine of summer.

The wheat fields would lie brown and bare, and apparently lifeless, until autumn arrived once more. Then Dad would drill winter wheat, the bleak fields would green up, and the cycle would start again.

13

From Heat and Dust to Floods and Blizzards

The weather ruled our lives and all of our activities. Newspaper headlines had little impact on us—the assassinations of Kennedy and King, the war in Viet Nam, race riots in Detroit. We were affected by droughts in Russia and trade agreements with China. Whenever we stepped outside, we automatically looked up to the sky to check for a hint of an approaching storm. The weather forecasts had precedence over anything else on TV. My father seemed to take a long dry spell calmly, stating only that we'd get some rain when we needed it, but I knew he was anxious about the wheat that would shrivel in the head if moisture didn't come, and about the dry land milo that would become thin and stunted.

When the weather came on, however, he ignored the TV, and continued reading the market report in the newspaper. But if the weatherman pointed out a disturbance down in New Mexico, then the newspaper snapped down, and Dad stared intently at the screen and I knew we were likely to get something. A storm usually began as a few non-descript clouds low to the horizon in the south and west. Then thunderheads would build and build, towering into the sky, shining dazzling white. They appeared as solid and massive as mountains. Gradually, their tops flattened, and their undersides darkened, and a low mutter of thunder encouraged us.

Sometimes we would get what all the farmers wanted, a steady, soaking rain that meant Dad would spend the day working in the shop. If there was nothing there to keep him busy, he would sit inside the house, reading from a stack of farm magazines, and looking out of place to my brother and me. Not even when he was sick did he stay inside. Periodically he would toss his magazine aside, and stroll to the door where he stood and chuckled to himself as he watched the rain dripping from the eaves above the front porch. Soon the phone would start to ring as the neighbors called around to see how much had fallen.

More often than not, it would be a violent thunderstorm that ripped leaves and branches from the trees and lashed the rain horizontally against the house and cracked hailstones on the windows. Such a storm would flatten the green wheat, but it would rebound in a day or two. It could recover two times, Dad said, but after a third time it wouldn't rise again, and it would be harder to cut.

I saw my mother crying once after such a storm. Her tears alarmed me; I had never seen her cry before and would not again until she lay dying of cancer. I did not understand when she choked out that the hail had ruined the ripe wheat that was almost ready to cut. I went back to collecting the chunks of ice scattered about on the withered buffalo grass and wondered if I could store some in the freezer. To the east, a rainbow glowed against the black clouds, and the air smelled fresh and clean, but the stalks of wheat hung bent and broken.

Other times the huge thunderheads that looked so promising produced only a brief spatter, and the erratic storm would move on to dump an inch of rain just a mile or two away, teasingly leaving us with only some cooler air. At night I watched the lightning illuminating the clouds, flashing from one heavy mass to another,

The Farm on the Wall

as though a war was being waged. The thunder was too far away to be heard. I would report to Grandpa when he called that we got just enough to settle the dust, a phrase we repeated throughout the summer months. The irrigation wells were kept running day and night to pump water to the thirsty corn, and we went back to watching the sky and hoping.

The weather would go in cycles of wet years, and dry years, though it always seemed to me that there were more dry years than wet years. 1951, though, was a wet year—a catastrophic flood year, to be more accurate. May, June and July of 1951 saw record rainfalls over most of Kansas and Missouri. "The June 1951 monthly average rainfall over Kansas of 9.55 inches was the greatest monthly average ever recorded."[1] In July, there was a tremendous burst of rain over four days—about 17-19 inches fell in the eastern part of the state, and the overloaded Kansas, Marais Des Cygnes, and Neosho Rivers sent walls of water downstream that devastated Manhattan, Topeka, Lawrence, Kansas City, and other towns.

Some 45,000 homes were destroyed or damaged, and highways and railroads were closed for weeks. In Kansas City, locomotives were driven onto 17 bridges to keep them from washing away, but the weight of the water was too much and they were lost. Animals were washed away from the famous stockyards, which never recovered. Elsewhere in eastern Kansas, thirty-three water-supply systems were shut down. The force was such that some of the streams changed course and their channels were widened. By today's standards, the damages amounted to $17 billion.[2]

Even in southwest Kansas it was a wet spring, Dad said; all the ditches, mud holes and swales—the shallow depressions in fields that stayed somewhat marshy—were full of water. The Gordon Soddy to the west of the farm dissolved in the standing water, and the surviving daughters had no place to go until rescued by the Red Cross. Low spots on the roads flooded over, and farmers had to drive carefully so they didn't stall the engine in their pickup. The constant rains had washed out the Winkler milo three times, and they had to wait for the fields to dry out so they could replant.

Carol Winkler Kotsch

My father and Grandpa were moving tractors from one field to another that spring. Dad was in front and Grandpa followed behind, when they came to a large section of road—about fifty yards—that was flooded over out into the fields. Dad could not tell where the edge of the road dropped off into the ditch, so as he slowly entered the muddy water, he was careful to keep his eye on the road where it reappeared up ahead, and drive in a straight line.

Finally, he made it through, but when he turned around to check on his father, he was startled to see that my grandpa's tractor was off the road and leaning over in the ditch. Carefully, Dad backed up his tractor until he reached Grandpa, who was fuming at himself as he took off his boots and socks, rolled up the legs of his pants, and helped Dad hook a chain onto his tractor so Dad could pull it out of the ditch.

I laughed, thinking of my careful grandpa getting a tractor stuck in a water-filled ditch in the driest part of Kansas. How had it happened? *Oh, said Dad, your grandpa got to watching the waves ripple across the water, and was so hypnotized that he got seasick, and followed them right across the road and down into the ditch.* When the ground dried out later that year, Grandpa had the hill north of the farm terraced to prevent erosion during the next wet year.

1952 was another wet year, though not as much. Across the state, construction was planned for a series of reservoirs and levees to prevent another such flood. Still, there was enough rain, that when your father was born that April in Kansas, his family had to use a rowboat to get across one of the flooded roads to their home in Wyandotte County.

Eventually, the rains fell less and less, and the rest of the Fifties were dry by the time my parents were married in '55. Wet years returned in due course, but farmers were beginning to depend on irrigation wells to increase their yields. The Ogallala Aquifer, which ran through Nebraska, Kansas, Oklahoma and Texas, was not far below the surface, and after World War II, when rural areas got electricity, farmers could afford to dig wells and have a reliable source of water.

The Farm on the Wall

 The irrigation well up the hill was close by to the foundations of Auntie and Uncle's old house, and the motor's growling purr vibrated in the air every spring and lasted all summer. After a while, I no longer noticed it. Even at night it only lulled me to sleep. The water was pumped up from nearly 200 feet and was cold and sweet. Dad would plow a ditch about three feet deep along the edge of the field. Then he would walk along and drape long, slender, s-shaped siphon tubes over the edge of the ditch to catch the water and suck it up and over and down the rows of wheat.

 Once I was allowed to wear my swimsuit when we went up the hill to check the water, and Dad let me paddle in the ditch. I sank nearly to my knees in the mud and shivered in the cold water, though it must have been a blazing hot Kansas day. Eventually the siphon tubes were replaced with 30-foot sections of aluminum irrigation pipe, which I would sometimes help put in place, though Dad did most of the work. In the evenings I would make the rounds with him and turn on the gates to let the water run down the furrows.

 F.M. Luther's 1911 pamphlet had declared "there is a great sheet of pure water of inexhaustible supply all over the county,"[3] and well drillers told Dad there would always be plenty of it, but eventually, farmers began pumping out more water than seeped back down to the aquifer, and they had to dig their wells increasingly deeper to bring up enough to keep the land producing. Finally, the well "over west" on a half section three miles from our farm went dry, and Dad had to go back to dry land farming there.

 In the winter we waited for snow to cover the wheat and insulate it from the south wind that would turn it dry and brittle. If it had been dry that fall, the dust would begin to blow. Then Dad might have to plow several deep furrows from east to west to bring up clods and act as a windbreak to catch the blowing dirt and stop the soil from being stripped away. After that, all we could do was wait and pray for moisture. Day after day the wind blew, filling our eyes with grit when we stepped outside, and roaring in our ears. *It's blowing something up,* Dad declared. When I went

Carol Winkler Kotsch

to check on the calves, the wind pushed me across the farmyard, but when I turned around, I had to lean forward almost double to get back inside the house.

And then the next day the wind stopped; the sun shone gently, and the sky was clear blue and calm. I could go outside without being swept off the steps to do my chores and play. The air was chilly, but I turned my face to the sun and felt the mild warmth. *It's a weather breeder*, Dad declared one evening, and he pointed out the sun dogs in the west, two bright spots in the sky on either side of the setting sun that were edged in red. The sunlight was reflecting off ice crystals high in the atmosphere, he told me, and that meant we were going to see a change. When we checked on the cattle, they were running and bucking about in the corral instead of quietly chewing their cud. I was puzzled over their unusual behavior, but Dad explained that they felt the change in the air pressure from an approaching storm, and that we might see snow in the morning.

The best snow to get was a heavy, wet fall that draped the wheat like a blanket; it would melt slowly and soak deep into the soil to act as a reservoir as the wheat revived and started growing again in the spring. It also added nitrogen to the soil—poor man's fertilizer, Dad called it. Quiet snowfalls were rare, and I would watch in wonder at the large flakes floating down and stacking up several inches high on fence posts and tree branches.

At other times, blizzards snapped the utility poles, and I would do my schoolwork by the flickering light of the old kerosene lantern that my grandparents had used before electricity reached the farm in the late 1940s. Big cities had been using electricity for decades, and even small towns had power—Montezuma obtained a municipal power plant in 1921 and turned on the lights on December 13[4]—but rural Kansas had to wait until 1938, as power companies didn't think it was worth the expense to string lines for miles on rough dirt roads to reach a small customer base. The Rural Electrification Administration was passed in 1935, which made loans to cooperatives seeking to provide power to rural areas. Farmers paid $5 for a hookup, "a sum not to be taken lightly

The Farm on the Wall

in those days."[5] The farms in Brown and Atchison counties were the first to receive power—a historical marker noting the first REA project was placed just outside Horton.

Gradually, 38 other cooperatives followed, and electricity reached every rural area.[6] Now farm families could exchange their Delco systems, gasoline generators that could furnish enough power for a radio and a couple of light bulbs, for unlimited, dependable power, and be relieved of some of their daily drudgery.[7] Grandpa, however, continued to rely on the farm's light plant and wind charger for several more years; the REA didn't make it out west until 1948, when Dad and Grandpa wired the house and some of the farm buildings. The cost was $10 a month for 200 kilowatts.

Once or twice we were without power for two or three days, eating lunchmeat sandwiches and cold cereal and milk, as we could not cook on the electric stove. Mom fretted over the contents of the freezer and the lack of hot coffee. Though it seemed exciting and adventuresome at first, going without electricity for a day or two quickly became dull and dreary, as the gray, overcast day stretched on and on with nothing to do but listen to the wind howling outside, and whining through the cracks of the house. The gas furnace kept the house warm, but electricity powered the water supply, so my brother and I cheerfully did without baths until the lights came back on, at least until we were teenagers. The toilet, though, had to be flushed from time to time with melted snow.

If Dad had cattle pastured out in the field when the blizzard hit, they would simply turn their heads away from the relentless, stinging gale, and walk over fences now covered by snowdrifts that were packed hard and solid by the wind as they sought refuge from the storm. When the wind stopped and the skies cleared off, Dad would start calling other farmers, describing his missing cattle and the Winkler brand to discover where they had wandered. Then he loaded up Chief in the horse trailer and set off to find and rope the cattle, which might be a few miles away, huddling in another farmer's windbreak, or sheltering in the hills by Meade, over 20 miles off to the south. Chief and Dad would spend a long afternoon churning through the snow to round up the exhausted, hungry cattle and haul them home.

Once the storm was over, I wandered down to the pasture, walking on top of the snow-packed ditches, the drifts sculpted by the wind into sharp-edged, fragile curves. My red rubber boots crunched through the snow, though all other sounds were muffled and deadened. I turned my toes in and out to make unusual patterns that must have made some passing farmer smile when he glanced at the ditch. If the sun was shining, the light would dazzle my eyes and I would complain of a headache later to Mom. Sometimes I sank up to my hips where it had not crusted over enough to bear my weight. Then my boots, which were never meant to do more than splash in rain puddles, filled with snow and my feet would ache with the cold. If we had several days of bitter weather, the pond would freeze, and I would spend the afternoon sliding over the ice, knowing if it broke, the water would barely cover the tops of my boots.

The snow always drifted high on the north side of the long shed, stopping just a foot or two from the edge of the roof. I would hoist myself up from the drift onto the ice-glazed roof, and carefully pick my way to the top, where I could look down over the farmyard. There were my footprints, and the dog's, as well as pickup tracks left by Dad on his way to check the cattle and work in the shop. The brooder house would be empty now, as the last of the flock had been butchered when the hens stopped laying during the cold weather. Then I would bend over low and slide down the corrugated tin roof like an alpine skier to land on the drift and roll down the slope, taking care to avoid the electric fence that gave the cattle a shock if they tried to slip under it.

A good, heavy snow was a mixed blessing; it protected the wheat and provided moisture but stressed the cattle as they stood huddled behind the windbreak and caused them to lose weight. When it melted, the corral became a sea of mud and manure; Dad poured concrete slabs around the feed bunks, so they had something solid to stand on. If the snow persisted, all he could do was to make sure they had plenty of feed and wait for the weather to change once more.

14

Milk, Beef, and Pork

The barn you see in the picture and used to play in yourselves when we visited your grandparents is not the original building. The first one was south and west of that barn, and burned down, Dad said, destroying the hay and one or two of the horses and most of the harness. A neighbor, Barney Koehn, noticed a man walking across the field west of the house, and after that saw smoke and flames. It might have been a drifter seeking shelter, they thought, who tossed out a cigarette, but they never knew.

Losing the barn was more of a blow than the loss of the horses and the equipment. There was probably no insurance, Dad thought, but a new barn was still necessary. Grandpa and Uncle built the current one sometime after Grandpa returned from the service in 1919. It was smaller than the first one, as they no longer needed as many horses. Trucks and tractors were taking over.

My grandparents had always kept a few cows to milk for the family's consumption, and to sell cream, but the dairy herd didn't get started until 1942 when the air base opened at Dodge City, and the enlisted men needed fresh milk. It was a small herd, only

Carol Winkler Kotsch

25 cows, but a milking machine was necessary, and that required electricity. Grandpa and Uncle installed a gas generator, and for the first time, the barn had electric lights that replaced the kerosene lamps and gas lights that had to be pumped with an air pump every thirty or forty minutes.

The milk that Grandpa and Uncle collected was stored in ten gallon cans and placed in the cooling tank inside the milk house, which was built at about that same time. It was dark and windowless, and the thick walls kept out the fierce heat of the summer. The milk truck from Fairmont Creamery made the rounds two to three times a week and collected the milk and took it to Dodge City where it was processed.

When Uncle Lowell was drafted in March of 1945, and left the farm to go the Philippines where he helped keep order after the war, his absence made it hard for Grandpa and Uncle and Dad to continue milking. Besides, the war was winding down and the air bases were empty. Twenty-two Jersey and Holstein cows, a few calves and a couple of young pigs were auctioned off a month later, along with the milking machine, the cream separator, and the milk pails. Grandma must have been doing some spring cleaning, for the newspaper notice also mentions household goods and miscellaneous articles.

Dad did not miss the dairy herd. He and his family could never travel very far from home as the cows had to be milked twice a day, and always at the same time, or they wouldn't produce as well. The discarded milk cans and crates were scattered around the farm in various buildings, used to prop up other implements or collect dust in a corner. The old milking stool was wedged into a crack in the walls of the granary; it looked like a piece of scrap lumber and stayed there for sixty years until Dad noticed it and tugged it out. The milk house was left empty, but years later, my brother and I dragged bits of cast-off furniture inside and used it for a playhouse.

The barn was my favorite place to play. It was dim and hushed after coming in from the blinding heat of mid-day; dust motes drifted upward through the rays of sun that slipped through the cracks of the loft door. The dusty scent of hay would give me sneezing fits later. Sometimes a barn owl would take up residence in the loft and we would startle each other as I came up the ladder. A constant supply of barn cats lived there too and produced many litters of kittens they hid carefully away behind the bales of hay. They were always wild and shy at first, but I lured them out by imitating the sound of their mother and bringing them scraps snatched from the kitchen. The bales of hay made good forts and my father didn't seem to notice how his neat stacks had been rearranged. Later, when I discovered Greek mythology, the bales formed the ramparts of Mt. Olympus, and dried milo stalks became thunderbolts hurled from on high.

It was empty of the familiar Jersey and Holstein cows when I played there, but their stalls and calving pens still stood inside the barn and penciled on their sides were tally marks Grandpa and Uncle had made. Though the workhorses that had plowed the fields and harvested the wheat had been gone for many years, bits of old bridles still hung from nails, along with a horseshoe or two. The wall cupboard was filled with the crumbling nests of mud daubers and barn swallows, and a few old-fashioned, heavy glass bottles still containing an inch or two of mysterious liquids to treat an ailing cow. A metal sign proclaiming, "We use DeLavel Milking Machines" hung on the outside of the barn. You can't make it out in the picture, girls, but it hung right underneath the loft door.

The cattle on our farm were raised for beef. Every fall, Dad bought stock that was hauled up from Texas in semi-trucks. Unlike most of the surrounding farmers, he always bought heifers, as they were $22 to $23 per hundred pounds compared to steers, which might cost $30 per hundred pounds. Steers would put on more weight—two pounds a day, compared to one and a half for a heifer—but Dad found he could sell his heifers for about four-fifths of what a steer brought.

Once unloaded, the scared and confused cattle would mill about in the corral next to the house, mooing themselves hoarse and keeping us awake through the night. After a few days, when

Carol Winkler Kotsch

they had settled down, branding would begin. I was careful to keep my distance from the portable gas furnace where the branding iron was heating up. It looked like a small metal barrel turned on its side and standing on four thin iron legs. The propane gas hissed and rumbled and I could glimpse the upside-down JI brand glowing red-hot. Sometimes I would be the assistant, handing Dad the de-horning saw; or the syringe and a bottle of medicine; or a thumb-sized pill and the injector. What I really liked to do was help run the cattle through the loading chute, but Dad worried that a panicked cow might trample me. He himself was missing the nail from his big toe when a frantic heifer charged him, and once, while trying to give an injection, his hand was jostled by a bucking cow, and the needle gouged his thumbnail.

Each animal was inspected for illness or injury and given an injection as needed. Dad would keep an eye on those heifers over the next few days in case they needed to go into the sick pen for special treatment. I noticed something odd about the eyes on one of the heifers as they were going through one year and called Dad over to look at the strange bumps on the eyelids. He was puzzled as well as we both stared; the heifer didn't seem to be bothered by them. Then we looked closer and realized the bumps were ticks, picked up somewhere in the Texas scrub; the hairless eyelids were the easiest place for them to attach themselves. Dad reached for the ever-present pliers on his belt, and pulled them off, one by one. We found them on several other heifers that day, but never came across them again.

Horns were cut off first, so the heifer couldn't use them to bully the other cattle out of their share of feed. They dropped off cleanly most of the time, and the dog snatched them up to chew, but occasionally, the de-horner bit too deep, and then Dad would be sprayed in the face by the spouting artery as he struggled to cauterize it and cover the wound with dehorning powder.

After each heifer had been doctored, then Dad thrust the branding iron through the bars of the chute and held it to the animal's left flank for a few seconds. I could hear the flesh sizzle and smell the burned hair and hide. The terrified animal bellowed in pain and rolled its eyes as it jerked and struggled to get away, making the iron bars of the loading chute rattle and clank. Then the chute clanged open, and it burst out, shaking its head in bewilderment and looking for the rest of the herd. A scab would form in a few days, and fall off, and the cattle would be turned out on winter wheat, or to clean up the stubble from the corn harvest.

Sometimes they needed a little extra to supplement their grazing out behind the barn. Dad would toss a couple of hay bales in the back of the pickup, unhook the gate to the electric fence, and drive my brother and me out on the winter wheat. The cows knew what was coming, and did not run off, but slowly began to line up and follow the pickup.

Then Dad would shift the gear down as low as it would go into "grandma," and tell us to keep it headed straight. He hopped out the door and jumped up onto the bed, while one of us slid over behind the wheel to steer. We could just barely see over the top of the steering wheel but managed to keep the pickup on a straight heading as it lurched slowly and steadily over the furrows. Sometimes Dad would holler at us to turn left or right, and then it felt as if we were really driving, though our feet did not reach the pedals. When the hay was all scattered, then Dad jumped out, caught up with the truck, and slid back in.

When the corrals were empty and quiet again, Dad would produce five to seven young calves and pen them in a corner. My brother and I took care of them, checking twice a day to see that they had water and feed. It was a pleasant chore after school in the fall, scooping up a can full of molasses-laced grain to drizzle in the feed bunks and then topping it with several flakes of hay that we dragged from the barn. I wished I were strong enough to carry a bale of hay the way Dad did, swinging it along with one hand and just barely leaning to the side.

It was harder to go outside early on a dark winter morning to check on our calves when the wind was blowing strong from the north. Now I had to stop and crack open the ice-covered stock tank with the ax, and then fish out the bobbing pieces with the pitchfork. Sometimes the corral would be littered with cinderblock-sized chunks for weeks until the temperature climbed above freezing. I hurried inside when I was done to warm up before the school bus pulled in, and to pick out the prickly wheat beards from my coat.

We looked after those calves diligently, never missing a day, and it paid off when it was time to haul them to the McKinley-Winter sale barn in Dodge City, along with Dad's cows. Outside, the parking lot was crowded with muck-smeared semi-trucks and horse-trailers, and crooked rows of pickups, some shiny and new, others faded and mud-crusted. Inside, it smelled of manure and hay and tobacco smoke. We climbed through the tiered rows of wooden folding seats that encircled the sale ring, where sale hands flicked their whips over the backs of skittish cows and steers as they were herded in and out of the ring for the buyers to inspect. Dad warned us not to wave our hands around in case the fast-talking auctioneer would mistake our innocent nose-scratch for a bid, so my fearful brother and I kept our elbows tight to our sides.

I found the auctioneer's chant impossible to follow as he swung quickly about from side to side, acknowledging ranchers and cattle buyers as they flicked the brim of a go-to-town cowboy hat, or nonchalantly raised a finger. The background murmur of the barn stopped as he focused on the serious bidders: *Who'llgivemeeighteen-eighteen-eighteen-eighteenandahalf-I'mbideighteenandahalf-eighteenandahalf-eighteenandahalf-who'llmakeitnineteen-nineteen-nineteen-I'mbidnineteen-nineteen-nineteen-nineteenandahalf-nineteenandahalf-I'vegotnineteenandahalf-who'llmakeittwenty...*

Faster and faster he went, back and forth, pointing demandingly from one to the other, louder and louder, until bang! The hammer went down and the cattle were sold. Then the murmurs started up again as the on-lookers discussed the price and the buyer and the quality of the cattle.

The bidders themselves seemed oblivious to the drama, keeping their faces expressionless so a competitor and the auctioneer could not guess how much they were willing to spend. Dad pointed out our calves as they were paraded around the ring, but I could not tell how much they made until we went down to the front office and picked up the bill of sale. The profits from six of the calves would be divided between us and deposited into our college accounts, but Dad would keep what the seventh calf made, to pay for the grain and hay we used.

Sometimes one of Dad's heifers would unexpectedly produce a calf—a "coupon", he called it—and he would tuck them away in the barn for a few weeks. I would watch in delight as one sucked at its mother's udder, the tiny tail swishing back and forth, slowly at first, and then speeding up as the milk came down, reminding me of a windshield wiper. Afterwards it would caper around the tiny pen, kicking up its heels and bouncing up and down.

There was a Black Angus calf born one year, which Dad promptly called Rastus, a name he said was given to all black calves kept in the barn. I didn't learn until years later that it was a derogatory nickname and one I could not use in public, though I didn't understand why. Dad kept Rastus and his mother penned in the barn overnight and then turned the cow out to graze all day with the rest of the herd on the winter wheat growing behind the barn. Late in the afternoon, when I got home from school, I would open the door to the barn, and do my best to bawl like a calf in the direction of the cattle. The anxious cow charged up, and I was careful not to get between her and her calf, which was by now bawling for his mother himself.

The cow always faced me as she nursed her calf. Rastus had grown used to my constant visits and would let me scratch his ears, but his mother remained suspicious of my presence. I stood quietly on the other side of the Dutch door, hands outstretched, hoping she would eat the grain I was holding. Not until I dropped the grain would she approach, and then only after I had backed away. I brought the grain day after day, until finally she stepped up hesitantly and ate from my hands. I stood as still as still, hardly believing it had happened. Rastus raced around the stalls, his tail stretched out straight behind him. When the cow was finished, she sniffed at my face and gave it a lick.

Carol Winkler Kotsch

Before Dad took his cattle to market, he would set aside one of the heifers to grain feed in the corral for several weeks. Then he loaded it up into the horse trailer and hauled it to a local beef processor to be butchered. All year long I ate roast beef and T-bone steaks without a second thought, never thinking how we were envied by town and city dwellers. But it wasn't always so, even for my grandparents. Until A. P. Bargar added meat lockers to his ice-making plant around 1934, they ate lots of fried chicken during the summer, and had ham and sausage from the previous fall, but very little beef. Grandma killed, picked and cleaned two chickens two or three times every week of the summer to feed the family. She also made some kind of cheese pie, Uncle Lowell remembered, something like a cheesecake, only savory, but chicken was the main meat until fall when butchering could begin.

When cold weather arrived in November and December, and could be expected to last, Great-Grandpa and Grandma Graves, Grandma and Auntie's parents, showed up to help butcher hogs for summer use. Up to four hogs might be killed, cleaned, and cut over the next couple of days. After a hog was shot between the eyes, Grandpa unhooked the singletree from the plow, where it hung from the hitch. This was an oak bar about three feet long, which helped balance the motion of the horses as they swung from side to side while plowing or pulling a wagon. He hung it by its center loop to a tripod set up in the doorway of the shed. The pig's back legs went through the hooks at both ends where the traces of the harness for the workhorses normally went, and then Grandpa and Uncle used a chain hoist to gradually pull the pig up until the head was off the ground, and slit the pig's throat.

When the blood was drained, the hog was lowered into a long vat filled with scalding hot water in order to soften the bristles. Then it was lifted out and pulled up onto a flat table next to the vat. Great-grandpa Graves and Grandpa began to scrape off the hairs. The pig was pulled up once more away from the table, and then Grandpa took his butchering knife and made a long slit from the tail to the head, and the intestines tumbled out. The liver was saved, but the rest was hauled off to the draw, the shallow depression west of the barn, for the coyotes to scavenge. The hams, shoulders, and bacon were cut out, and any scraps saved for sausage.

The fat was sliced off and cut into small chunks, and tossed into the rendering kettle, where a slow, steady fire was burning so the lard wouldn't scorch. Grandma and Great-Grandma Graves had to watch it carefully and stir it constantly. When all the fat was rendered out, the cracklings, the leftover crispy bits, were strained off to be eaten as a treat for later.

The hams, shoulders, and bacon were placed on a table in the basement, and Grandpa rubbed them all over with a mixture he called Hickory Salt to cure the meat with a hickory flavor and draw off the moisture. Every couple of days, he would turn the meat over and rub them all over again. After about two to three weeks, family members took their share and the rest was wrapped in paper and hung in the basement.

The sausage grinder was hauled out, and pork scraps fed through it and ground. Grandma shaped it into patties, fried them, and then stacked them into stoneware crocks. Hot lard was poured over the patties until they were covered. As the lard cooled and hardened, it acted like a lid and prevented bacteria from growing and spoiling the meat. When Grandma wanted some sausage, she dug it out of the lard, fried out the grease, and served it to her family. A fresh layer of lard was poured on to preserve the remaining pieces.

Grandpa added some lye to the rest of the lard, cooked it and left it to cool. After it hardened, it was cut into pieces and ready to be used as soap. On Monday mornings, he would get a coal fire going in the stove, and then placed a tub of water on top of one of the two burners. While the water was heating, Grandpa shaved strips of soap. When the water was hot enough, he dissolved the soap into the tub, and then poured it into Grandma's hand-wringer washing machine. It got the grease and dirt out, Uncle Lowell recalled, but it didn't take many washings for the harsh lye soap to fade their clothing.

Grandpa also butchered a steer in the winter. Like the pigs, it was shot in the head and the carcass hauled up on the singletree. As the steer was pulled up, Grandpa and Uncle would skin it and pull down the hide, cutting it off at the head. It would be salted and rolled up and sold the next time the family made a trip into Montezuma.

Then the steer was gutted and cut in half. The liver and heart were saved for the family to eat, but everything else was discarded, except the bladder, which would be blown up for Dad and Uncle Lowell to kick around the farmyard. Some of the meat was cut off and cooked and canned for the summer months, but the rest of the carcass was covered with a sheet, and hoisted up high in the granary with a rope and pulley where it hung, frozen solid, until Grandma wanted some meat. Then Grandpa lowered it across a couple of sawhorses and cut off enough to thaw for supper the next day.

Once meat lockers became available, the carcass was eased down onto sheets lining the newly-washed pickup bed, cut into quarters and driven into Montezuma, where it was further cut and wrapped and frozen. Once a week Grandpa would visit the locker the Winkler family rented and pick out the cuts Grandma had written on her list. Now a week's worth of meat could be stored in the small freezer in the refrigerator at home and taken out at her leisure.

Grandpa continued to help Dad with the butchering once or twice after he retired, in return for a share of the meat. He entered the house triumphantly after finishing slaughtering with Dad one afternoon, holding aloft a pan, and announcing that he had saved my favorite for supper that night. Then he tilted the pan to show me a fresh cow's tongue, which I loved better than roast beef.

Until Dad and Mom added a deep-freezer to the basement, we continued to pick up a week's supply of meat along with the groceries we bought in Montezuma. Air-conditioning was still rare, so walking into the sparkling, frost-covered locker was always a welcome shock, but soon I was hopping back and forth in my bare feet, trying to keep warm as Dad picked out the pieces Mom wanted. Beefy, the butcher, mailman, and son-in-law of the original grocer, liked to tease me by threatening to lock me in. I stayed close to Dad, knowing he was teasing, but still afraid of being left behind in the cramped, dark locker.

Once we had our own deep freezer, fresh meat was easily fetched to the kitchen. I was spoiled by the abundance of steaks and roasts and longed for shrimp, a rare delicacy, and one that seemed as exotic as the Chinese food served to daring diners at the Silver Spur in Dodge. Every now and then, Dad had a taste for brains, which the processor would save at his request. They sat in the refrigerator, a mass of pinkish-gray wrinkles. My brother and I would surreptitiously open the door to stare at them and shudder. Dad had to cook and eat them by himself; Mom wouldn't touch them, and I lacked the courage to try them.

The iron rendering kettle was no longer needed, but lurked about in the farmyard, too heavy to be easily moved, and too awkward to play with. One day Dad did some measuring, got out his welder, and turned it into a grill. It cooked hamburgers quite well, and the neighbors joined us for a barbeque.

15

Horses Return to the Farm

On the last day of second grade, as the school bus pulled into our driveway to drop us off for the summer, I was astounded to see a horse in our corral. I could hardly get out of the bus fast enough. Dad had bought a horse to rope and move cattle. His name, I was told, was Chief. He was a big, good-natured sorrel gelding with a blaze down his nose and four white stockings. I could not reach the top of his back as he stood about sixteen hands tall and had the build of a workhorse. Though his gaits were rough for pleasure riding, he could be depended on to dig in and hold steady after Dad had roped a calf and dismounted to doctor it.

  At first, Dad would hoist me up behind Mom and we would trot up the hill and back, my head bouncing around until I thought it would snap off. Then, as time passed, Mom would let me sit in the saddle by myself after she had ridden Chief enough to take the edge off him. Though my feet barely reached the stirrups, she led me around the barnyard, teaching me to post to the trot. It was hard at first to coordinate pushing up from the stirrups in rhythm to the horse's gait, but I persisted, and soon I was able to move along smoothly with the horse. When Mom and Chief went out for a ride, I would watch by the window for their return, and would be bitterly disappointed if Chief stumbled home covered with lather, too tired to trot around the shed with me. I could only help brush his sweaty sides and legs with the currycomb and hope for the next time.

I seized the chance to slip up onto Chief one day while Mom was bent over in the garden pulling weeds. He was standing by the corral fence which bordered the garden, head hanging down, ears slack, and eyes half closed; only his tail lashed about in short bursts to shoo away flies. I climbed the fence and dropped down on his back. Chief shook himself and began walking about the corral. Grasping his mane in both hands, as I knew the Indians did, I sat up straight and proud. We hardly had time to circle the corral before Mom looked up and screamed. Chief ambled back to the fence, and I climbed down, wondering at Mom's white face.

As I improved, I was allowed to ride Chief by myself. I had to stand in the feed bunk in order to slip the hackamore over his head, and then I grabbed his mane and the reins, and threw my legs over his back, which seemed as broad and wide as the kitchen table. The saddle was too heavy for me to handle on my own, but I had learned to cling to his bare shoulders with no trouble. I had strict instructions to go no farther than the corner and back, but only at a sedate trot, though I longed to be galloping around the section.

Chief was a trustworthy mount, but once his head was turned toward home and the feed bunk, he would break into a gallop and become impossible for me to stop. I hauled back on the reins with all the strength in my puny arms as we narrowly missed the utility pole, but even so, he didn't slow down until we came to the driveway, and then to the granary, where he stopped and waited to be brushed down and returned to the corral with a handful of grain.

Other times, I would let him graze at the fringes of the winter wheat that grew nearly to the edge of the farmyard. So calm was

The Farm on the Wall

he that I could stand on his broad back as he tore into the tender wheat or drape myself across his shoulders. Once, to Dad's displeasure, we rode through the wheat just as it was heading out. I didn't try to stop Chief when he broke into a canter, but rocked smoothly along on his back, listening to the muffled rhythm of his hooves and the swish of the wheat as we sailed through a sea of green. Then Chief stumbled, and I slid off, a long, long, way down, and landed with a teeth-jarring thump on clods of dirt. He pulled up in front of the shed, tossed his head, snorted, and looked around to see where I was with the currycomb and the grain.

When Dad added Missy to the farm, a two-year-old grade mare with a capricious disposition, then Mom and I rode around the countryside together, plowing into the wind, the dog panting along at our heels. I had my own boots to wear now, instead of making do with sneakers. We became a familiar sight to the farmers going down the road, though the righteous Mennonite ladies frowned, as we should have been at home, respectably sewing or baking.

Missy stood shorter than Chief, but was the same sorrel color, with a blaze on her nose. I noticed some odd, faint patches on her hindquarters that were slightly darker. Dad said it was a sign that she had some "Three Bars" in her background, referring to a famous Quarter horse stud known for siring first-class cutting and racing horses. Since grade horses weren't registered, we never knew, but Missy had the muscular, compact build of a Quarter horse, and excelled at cutting cattle. She could pivot so sharply to track a zigzagging calf that I nearly fell out of the saddle.

We usually went riding at the end of the day, when it had cooled down some, and Dad wasn't too busy to help us saddle up. Missy would trot steadily for miles, sometimes breaking into a smooth canter. With several nudges, she'd go full-out at a gallop—Dad said she sure could pick 'em up and put 'em down again. She walked so slowly, though, that Mom compared her to molasses in January, and only half-jokingly threatened to put a burr under the saddle. If Missy was tired of being ridden, she would unexpectedly duck her head to throw off an inattentive rider. Her wily personality meant I had to wait again until I was skilled enough to ride her instead of plodding old Chief.

She caught me off guard one day, and I went sailing over her ears to land on my back in the soft, plowed field; wheat stubble pricked my arms and neck. Then I opened my eyes to see Dad's anxious face; I was a little dazed and he was worried. I stood up shakily and went inside to doctor my scrapes and bruises. The next time I saddled up, I was ready for her. The instant she ducked her head, I pulled straight up on the reins with all the might in my right arm and grabbed the saddle horn with my left hand. The bit dug deep into her tender mouth, but Missy resisted, bucking and kicking.

Hang on, hang on! I vaguely heard my mother yell. *Ride her out!* Dad shouted. Somehow, I pulled harder, and Missy gave in and stopped. She had more respect for me after that, and though she tried again a time or two, her attempts were half-hearted, and I quickly squashed them.

When your grandmother rode, girls, she wore a cowboy hat and leather gloves, a denim jacket, and straight-leg jeans. Her back was ruler-straight in the saddle, and her boot heels pointed properly down in the stirrups. She held the reins securely in front of the saddle horn with her right hand; her left hand carried a riding bat, though she seldom used it. A sharp rap with it against her boot was usually enough to bring the horse in line. Her personality changed while on a horse, becoming assertive and authoritative; while I struggled to guide and control a stubborn mount, sometimes ending up backwards in the ditch, Mom was moving gracefully along. For a time, we even experimented with teaching the horses to jump over small stacks of railroad ties, though they were not at all enthusiastic.

We were devoted riders, and Dad added yet another horse to the corral—a registered Quarter horse gelding named Leo Prince, who came complete with papers and a high-strung, restless temperament from his racing ancestors. Chief stayed behind while Mom rode Leo, and I moved up to Missy. Leo, though, turned

The Farm on the Wall

out to be a handful, who needed serious ranch work to keep him occupied. He tossed his head constantly as we rode, and always seemed to be on the brink of bolting. Mom's arms ached from the constant effort to keep him under control; even a tie-down hooked from the bridle to the girth to keep him from throwing his head around was of little help. I was not allowed to ride him, and I noisily protested; I was positive that he and I would have an instant rapport if only I could get in the saddle.

One day, while Mom was busy in the house, and Dad was occupied in the shop, I stealthily made my way over to the corral. I did not dare go to the granary where the halters and saddles were kept, in case someone saw me come out with a bridle in my hands, but I had a plan. Slipping through the gate, I took off my new suede belt with the fringed end, and casually wrapped it around Leo's neck. He followed me quietly over to the feed bunk, and I threw my legs over his bare back, just like I used to do with Chief.

At first, he walked calmly around the corral as I guided him with my belt, but it didn't last long. He jumped suddenly, and lunged forward, ready to run, and I slid right off, tumbling through the manure, and just missing the feed bunks. I wasn't hurt—just bruised—but my clothes were stained and stinking, and now I had to sneak inside the house and change. The new belt was ruined, and I was no longer so anxious to ride him. Eventually, Dad decided Leo was too much for us to handle, and he was sold, and I went back to riding Chief alongside of Mom and Missy.

Mom was sure that Missy would throw a good colt if she was bred, so we took her to the Robertson brothers, Laverne and Junior, who dabbled in Quarter Horse racing, and had a registered stud at hand. I had to wait eleven long months for the result. In the final weeks, I was constantly back and forth from the house to the corral, checking on her a dozen times a day. At last I noticed that her udder had swollen, and was waxy and dribbling milk, and knew that she was close to foaling. A few days later, after many false alarms, I found her lying on the ground, and raced back inside, yelling for Mom.

We watched the front hooves appear, and then a nose, and

then things slowed down. Mom and I bent down to give her a hand, and with another push from Missy, tugged out a colt, just as Dad pulled up after being fetched from the field by my brother. I was dancing with excitement but managed to keep still and quiet so Missy could tend to her colt. She licked him from front to back, and he began to fumble with his legs as he struggled to stand. He reminded me of the daddy-long-legs spiders down in the basement as he tried to push himself up, managing to get the front ones under control, and then the hind legs, before they began to shake and wobble and he fell over to try again.

At last he was successfully on his feet, and began to nudge along Missy's side, searching for her udder. Whenever he nosed it, though, Missy would flinch and sidle away, and the colt would have to start again, moving clumsily on his still-shaky legs. She would not stand still to let him suck, and we were puzzled; Dad had us lead them into the barn for some privacy while he buried the afterbirth.

When we checked on them several hours later, Missy had still not let the colt nurse, despite her abundant udder. Dad called on Laverne for help. He arrived carrying a wooden handle with a loop of chain at one end, a twitch, he called it; I had no idea what it was used for. He looked Missy over and said her bag was swollen so tightly with milk that it hurt whenever the colt tried to suck. Once he started though, it would relieve the pressure, and the pain would be gone. The trick was to get Missy to stand still.

Laverne wrapped the loop of chain around Missy's sensitive upper lip and twisted the handle until it was just firmly attached. Now we waited for the colt to try again. When Missy tried to move away, Laverne twisted the handle tighter. Her attention was caught by the pain on her lip, and she stood still. Quickly, the colt began to suck, and Laverne eased off the tension. If Missy moved again, Laverne tightened the twitch until she was quiet.

The colt, named Sam, finished all his mother's milk; his sides were round, and Missy appeared to be relieved. We left them alone for the night, and in the morning, we found Sam sucking happily away, as Missy stood with one hip slack so he could reach

The Farm on the Wall

her udder easily. It was smooth sailing after that, and he grew quickly.

Mom and I broke Sam to wear a halter; we taught him to stop and go and back up while guiding him with a lead rope and got him used to the feel of a saddle pad on his back. We turned him over to some horse-breaking neighbors when he was a year old, and they kept him for several months, teaching him to carry a rider and go after cattle.

Sam became a superb cow horse, just as Mom had predicted. He was like a Rolls-Royce compared to faithful old Chief and could canter without effort for miles as we went around the section. Still, despite Mom's horsemanship, he ran away with her one day while I was at school. She was thrown and received a mild concussion, and after that she never rode again. We sold him to the neighbors, who let me borrow him any time I wanted a change from Missy. If Mom had any anxieties for me as I continued to canter down the road and around the section, she kept them to herself. Her riding boots gathered dust in the closet until I saved them for my own, many years later.

The money-making cattle, and the horses we used to look after them, had a superior status to the many dogs and cats that came and went over the years. They were pets, yes, but they were there primarily to guard the house and warn of visitors, and to catch rats and mice in the barn. The dogs ate their dog food out of the sack in the granary, while the cats had to make do with what they could catch, and my brother and I could sneak to them.

Their position changed, however, when we left for college, and the house became empty. Now the dog became Mom's companion while Dad was out in the fields. When I came home during break from college, I was startled to find her cutting up pancakes and dousing them with syrup, not for me, but for the dog. The cats came and went through a pet door in the garage where their brand-name cat food was kept, and no longer lived in the barn.

Of all the dogs who patrolled the farm, the most faithful and vigilant was Dusty, a German shepherd and collie mix who somewhat resembled a coyote. He was indeed covered with dust the day we brought him home, the only male in the neighbor's litter of puppies. Well-mannered and even-tempered, he trotted after us everywhere as we rode bikes and horses and moved cattle. His curved tail sliced through the wheat and weeds like a brown scythe as he sniffed out cottontails and rats.

Dusty took his guard duties seriously at night, barking and growling at unseen and inaudible intruders, until one of us, exasperated at the constant noise, would get up grumbling and drag him in. If he was still not satisfied he had scared off the trespasser, he would continue to bark indoors. It took Dad stomping out of the bedroom to make him stop, and then he would finally curl up in a corner, offended at our lack of appreciation for his watchfulness, and go to sleep. The coyotes in particular seemed to howl just to tease him. Wandering skunks ignored his warning barks, and he never learned to leave them alone, even after having been sprayed. The smell lingered for days, and he could not understand why no one would pet him.

Dusty even rode in the pickup with Dad whenever he went to check the irrigation wells and was sometimes mistaken for my mother by unsuspecting neighbors as they passed my father on the road. Dad always thought that with just a little training Dusty would make a good cow dog, as he seemed to have an instinct to herd cattle, but sometimes an irritated cow would charge him, and he would have to be closed up in the pickup, his nose glued to the window, whining urgently as he watched the cattle being moved without his assistance.

If Dad returned from a stop at a neighboring farm, Dusty's first act was to sniff the wheels to check for evidence of other dogs. Then he would cock his own leg and cancel out their mark. It was such typical dog behavior, that we didn't think twice about it, and had to remember to apologize to visitors from the city who weren't used to yellow stains on their tires. It was a habit, though, that got Dusty in trouble one day when he was riding along with Dad to check some cattle who were pastured in the winter wheat. They were kept in place with an electric fence, and most of them learned quickly to avoid leaning against it to reach something tasty-looking on the other side; even Dusty knew to keep his tail down when he ducked under the fence to chase a cottontail.

There was usually a stubborn heifer, though, who was willing to endure a shock or two to reach something greener, and the fence might be shorted out or knocked down as she leaned over to snatch a mouthful. Dad would check to see that the fence was still hot by driving the pickup up close enough so that the fender made contact. If he could hear a steady click..click..click over the radio, he knew the electricity was flowing. We were grounded, of course, inside the pickup, and knew better than to step outside while it was in contact with the fence.

But one day, Dad absent-mindedly opened the pickup door, and Dusty jumped right out. His first act was to sniff the tires, even though he had just inspected them a few minutes before. He cocked his leg as he always did, and then yelped in distress, thrashing and snapping at his unseen attacker. Instantly, Dad realized what had happened and backed up the pickup to break contact with the fence. There was nothing he could do for the dog, who was running in lopsided circles in the farmyard, but eventually, the shock wore off, and Dusty came back. Somehow, he understood the source of his pain, and ever after, if Dad was rolling up fence, or just picking up a length of wire, Dusty would growl and try to knock it away.

Mom was set against having a dog indoors, and so at first Dusty was only allowed in as far as the back porch in cold weather. If the door was left open, he would drape his head across the threshold and look pleadingly at us, his tail gently fanning the floor. Eventually, she relented, and he was allowed to sit on the rug in the kitchen. From there, it was an easy step to position his nose against the table as we ate, and quietly remind us of his faithful service. He soon had the run of the house, and Mother saved our leftovers for him.

Eventually, we had a turtle from Woolworth's, and a long-lived goldfish named Goldie, but I wanted something more exotic, a parrot, perhaps, or a hermit crab. I had a hamster, also from Woolworth's, and Grandpa and Grandma gave us rabbits one year; they were short-lived pets that escaped from their pen and were quickly snatched up by Dusty. We didn't blame the dog, knowing he was only following his instincts.

Dusty, though, remained our constant companion and confidant. He grew up along with us, though he turned grayer much sooner, and his joints began to ache with age. He could no longer keep up when Mom and I rode the horses, and we would have to close him indoors before we started. He kept vigil at the window, watching us go, and waited patiently for us to return. After many years, he could no longer go up and down the steps to get outside and began to whimper in pain. Dad could not bring himself to tell us for several weeks that Dusty had been put to sleep and was buried alongside the garden he had once guarded.

Missy was alone in the corral by now, and no longer had much of a purpose. Mom had stopped riding and Dad used a three-wheeler to check on the cattle or asked the neighbors to help. Dad continued to feed her, but finally took her to the sale barn while she could still be ridden and enjoyed by another generation.

16

Raising Chickens and Picking Vegetables

Early in March, when the wind blew thin and sharp and buffed my face, turning my face pink, and making my eyes water, and my nose run, Dad would clean out the debris from last year's chicken flock in the little brooder house. In the picture it's the small building just to the northeast of the house; a propane gas tank is next to it. Then he shoveled in clean sand and spread fresh straw. I poured meal in the chick-sized feeders and filled the little glass water fountain that looked like an upside-down Mason jar screwed into a circular tray. The gas heater was dragged in next, a metal contraption resembling a miniature octagonal circus tent with flaps at the base. The chicks would cluster under it to keep warm during the cool nights of early spring.

Fairmont Creamery supplied us with chicks shipped from Hutchinson and packed them in shallow cardboard boxes with perforated holes in the top, which my brother and I would diligently poke out later. One by one, I helped my father lift out the frantically cheeping chicks which scurried around the brooder house, filling our ears with their commotion. Gradually, they settled down as they found food and water, and began to scratch about. Later that night, Dad and I would return to the brooder house and check the temperature inside the heater through a side panel. When I peeked in, I could see the drowsy chicks huddled together and hear their sleepy peeps.

In just a few weeks, they would lose their soft, yellow down, and the pinfeathers would poke through, making them look like gangly teenagers. Now Dad hung the large chicken feeder from a hook on the ceiling and brought in the three-gallon fountain. It was my job every morning to pour in more feed if it was low, and make sure they had fresh water. The fountain had to be cleaned out every day, as the chickens filled it with straw and sand as they scratched. Mom saved all the vegetable scraps from the kitchen, and I would carry them over to their little run and toss them watermelon rinds and corn cobs and potato peels to peck at.

In my grandmother's day, the laying flock was kept in the chicken house catty-corner to the brooder house. My parents continued to keep a small flock there for a time, and in the evenings, I would layer straw in the bottom of the big metal can that once held grease, and help Mom gather eggs from the nesting boxes that lined the walls. It was always a chancy business reaching under a cold-eyed hen to snatch her eggs, and sometimes the anticipation of being pecked was worse than the actual event. If I wandered too close to the chicken house without Mom and Dad around, the belligerent rooster would chase me away, pecking at the backs of my legs as I ran screaming across the barnyard. I cheered when he ended up in the soup pot and gleefully devoured two helpings for supper.

Eventually, we stopped keeping a laying flock as we didn't need to rely on eggs and cream as my grandparents had, and the old chicken house was converted into a garage. The rows of nesting boxes were removed, and in their place, Dad set up a workbench and a welding station for farm implements, but we still continued to refer to it as the "chicken house."

The Farm on the Wall

When the baby chicks had filled out and weighed about three to four pounds, it was time to start butchering. Early in the morning, on a day when Dad had no other urgent work to do, and harvest was still a week or two away, the old chicken house-turned-garage was pressed into service for processing chickens for the freezer. Dad set up a makeshift table out of an old door and covered it with newspapers and started heating up water in a large metal bucket. Then he got out a long metal pole with a hairpin hook on one end, and a handle on the other—the "chicken catcher," we called it. He headed over to the brooder house, and I followed along, ready to do my part. Moving quietly so as not to panic the flock, Dad snagged three unsuspecting chickens by one leg with the hook, and handed two over to me to hold outside. The hens squawked in protest but couldn't do much hanging upside down.

Dad picked up the machete with one hand, placed a chicken's head against an old railroad tie with the other, and then the blade flashed down as I watched stoically. Dad could effortlessly hold the headless chicken in one hand as he waited for the blood to slow from a hissing spray down to a trickle, but my hands were not yet strong enough to keep the body from jerking loose and flopping about on the ground. When the body stopped its convulsions, he handed it over to me in exchange for a live one and repeated the process. Then I carried the now-limp bodies over to the old chicken house where Mom was waiting inside with knives and the washbasin.

The headless chickens were plunged into the bucket of hot water and scalded, and I began the tiresome business of plucking, holding the chicken with one hand, and ripping off the loosened feathers with the other, my arms and shoulders aching with the strain of holding up the dripping wet body. I always managed to miss some pinfeathers, for Mom frequently handed a carcass back to me to go over again.

When I learned to handle a knife, I graduated to cutting off the legs and wingtips, and then to cleaning out the body, sorting through the loops of intestines to cut out the gizzard and liver and heart. When I slit the gizzard open to clean out the grit, I would discover bits of glass the chickens had pecked up. Sometimes the young pullets would be close to laying, and we would find immature, shell-less eggs. These were set aside and added to the chicken noodle soup Mom made later. The flies became a real torment for us, stinging and biting with impunity, as we could not stop to swat at them, our hands deep in guts and feathers. Sometimes a particularly vicious one was impossible to ignore, and eventually we were speckled with dabs of blood from slapping at them.

Then Dad took the blowtorch and singed each gutted hen, making sure every last feather was gone. Mom slipped a heart, a gizzard and a liver back inside the body cavity. I packed them in heavy plastic bags for the freezer, Mom dunked them into the sink to push out all the air, and then we were finished, and it was time for the baloney sandwiches we always ate on butchering day.

The ten to twelve surviving chickens quickly forgot the earlier commotion and resumed their clucking and scratching. For the time being, they would provide us with fresh eggs. The young pullets laid erratically at first; sometimes the eggs were smaller than a ping-pong ball, others so large they had double yolks. Mom said they would settle down as they got older, and soon most of them were laying about an egg a day, brown and white.

After they were fed and watered, I left the door open so they could roam during the day. Though Dad had scattered a few old tires in the brooder house to serve as nests, some of the hens felt the call of old instincts and found hidey holes around the farm in which to lay. In the evening, I had to hunt through clumps of weeds and behind the scrap metal pile to discover where they were nesting and collect the eggs they had so carefully hidden. Some wandered into the long shed and fluttered their way up into a small grain bin. The hens decided that the oats made good nesting material and laid their eggs there but forgot about them. The eggs dried out over time, but when my brother and I found them, we discovered they made perfect bombs to throw at wasp nests. The eggs exploded with a satisfying pop and stink of sulfur, but we had to take off running from the furious wasps which would sting like fire if we weren't fast enough.

The Farm on the Wall

I washed and cleaned the eggs and stored them in leftover egg cartons. If there were more eggs than we could use, we sold them to relatives who visited, and I got to keep the money. The small flock would live on for a few more months, but their egg production slackened as the days got shorter, and eventually, they too, ended up on the table.

Grammie came with me once as I was checking the little flock, a chore she had performed countless times herself as a girl growing up on her family's farm in Troy, and later as a farm wife where I was now walking. She didn't accompany Grandpa and Uncle very often when they drove out from Dodge City to inspect the fields and see how the farm was doing without them. Perhaps she found it hard to look at the changes. Or perhaps it was painful to be reminded of the loss and struggles she had known. She was a tiny, white-haired lady who did not reach the shoulder of my almost six-foot Grandpa. I had grown tall enough to look over the top of her head.

I leaned to one side as I carried the heavy water fountain from the pump by the old chicken house back to the brooder house, and then Grandma and I stopped to listen to the hens as they clucked and crooned to themselves while scratching outside in the run. The glossy red rooster stretched out his neck, flapped his wings, and crowed loud and long, his head tilted back. To my astonishment, Grandma stood on tiptoe, stretched her neck, and crowed right back. I stared at her for a moment and tried to imagine her as a girl my age.

Mom had heard that ducks and geese would eat sandburs, so we tried raising some one year. We quickly discovered that they ate anything but sandburs, and left green splats everywhere, which put an end to bare feet. We didn't try them again but stuck with turkeys instead for a few years. When grown, the toms gobbled at any sound—the slam of a pickup door, a honking horn, a barking dog—and their red wattles turned blue as they shook their heads and spread their tail feathers to impress the hens. Nearly all their wild instincts had been bred out and they weren't very smart, but they stubbornly roosted on top of the brooder house at night, refusing to leave even during a violent thunderstorm, though Dad did his best to shoo them down. Dad sent them to the beef processor at butchering time and had them smoked; they were almost indistinguishable from ham, and our relatives looked forward to celebrating holidays with us.

Even chicken feed costs something, though, and the dropping price of fryers and eggs in the store didn't make it worth our time to continue to raise them. After I was gone from the farm, it was too labor-intensive for Mom and Dad to butcher by themselves, and soon the old brooder house was permanently empty.

Once the chicks were taken care of, then it was time for the garden. Robins didn't fly to our part of Kansas to let me know spring was near, but I could always count on the rhubarb to announce its arrival. I scanned the bare garden next to the corral, looking for the tightly wrinkled, yellow-green leaves poking out of the ground. Like my grandpa and father, I also had a taste for tartness, and when I spotted them, I rejoiced, for I could look forward to rhubarb pie for my birthday, a treat I considered superior to ordinary birthday cake. Mom even put candles on it for me. I tried eating a stalk right out of the garden, but it was too sour, even for me.

I knew if I found it sprouting down the hill, then I would be able to find Mom's old patch sprouting up the hill, where long ago, she and Dad planted some when they moved into Auntie and Uncle's old house. Sometimes Mom made a sauce of rhubarb and strawberries, and we ate it over ice cream, and I learned to make rhubarb crunch from the Mennonite cookbook in Mom's cupboard, but mostly we turned it into pies.

The asparagus planted by my grandparents still came up, and the spears followed soon after the rhubarb. Then it was time to get the rest of the garden ready for planting. My brother and I were called into service to load up the little red wagon with manure from the corral and spread it over the garden. The straw and manure from the chicken house was too hot for the garden, Dad said; the aged cow manure would break down better. We half-heartedly turned it over with shovels and were very glad when Dad got a roto-tiller to do the work for us. I can't remember that we ever did anything else to the garden; the soil was loose and loamy, and seeds sprouted without much care.

We planted potatoes and onions mid-March, with some radishes for me and a little lettuce for salads. Mom put in carrots and peas and green beans and cabbages, and when it was warmer, we added tomatoes and peppers, cucumbers, and zucchini. I liked planting the seeds well enough, and watching them sprout, but that was the easy part.

Weeds grew as quickly as the vegetables, and just as luxuriantly. Mom crawled on her hands and knees, pulling up each weed by the roots and tossing it into a bucket. I worked one row over, ripping off the tops, but missing the roots, and stabbing my fingers on goat-head stickers. My legs were covered with mosquito bites when I stood up. It was boring work, and I wandered off whenever possible.

Soon enough it was time to start picking the vegetables. Potatoes were fun—it was a little like digging for treasure as I pawed through the dirt looking for them—but I hated picking beans. My back ached as I bent over the endless rows, but Mom never complained. I cut off the ends of the beans and snapped them into smaller lengths. Then I brought up canning jars from the basement and counted rings and lids as Mom blanched the beans in hot water. She filled each Mason jar and put them in the pressure canner, four at a time. The kitchen became hot and steamy, and we spent the long afternoons counting the pings from the cooling jars as the lids contracted. If a lid did not pop, we knew it had not sealed properly, and had to be discarded, or bacteria would begin to grow. In a few days, more beans would be ready to pick and we would start all over.

We canned beans and tomatoes and carrots, froze corn, pickled the cucumbers, and made jam from strawberries. The potatoes were dug up, washed off and thoroughly dried so they could be stored without rotting. After the first frost, my brother and I gathered the unripe tomatoes still hanging on the dying vines, wrapped them in newspaper, and stored them in the basement to ripen. Once or twice, we traveled to the orchard at Fowler and

Carol Winkler Kotsch

picked peaches and pears to can. I sneaked them out of the bushel basket to eat on the way home and covered my face with itchy peach fuzz. All winter long, our summer produce was featured on the table.

Eventually, the effort and time required to can our vegetables was more than it cost to buy them already canned from the grocery store. We continued to plant a garden, though it was smaller now. Soon, the Mason jars stayed empty on the pantry shelves, and I found other uses for them.

17

Up and Down the Hill

I wandered all over the half section where the farm was, and up and down the hill, carrying with me the small white pocketknife I had found by the granary. I showed it to Dad and he thought perhaps it might have been the one he lost when he was a boy. The blade was speckled with rust, but still sharp, and I cleaned it up. I didn't use it much, except for whittling twigs, but kept it around, just in case.

Sometimes I followed one of the cow trails that fanned out from behind the barn. The boss cow decided where the herd would graze that day, and the rest obediently lined up behind her single file, their sharp hooves cutting a precise path that wove from side to side through the ankle-high winter wheat. I usually chose a trail that branched down to the draw, a depression northwest of the barn that was left unplowed for erosion control. It had become a dumping ground over the years, as Dad dragged the remains of trees that had failed to survive the Kansas weather there with the tractor. They made a natural jungle gym, and my brother

Carol Winkler Kotsch

and I would climb and swing through branches stripped smooth and white by the sun and wind.

Cattle the vet could not save were dragged there, too, and coyotes scattered their bones. My brother and I were confident that if we gathered up enough bones, we could reconstruct a skeleton, but the paper grocery sacks full of sun-bleached ribs and vertebrae in his bedroom gave him nightmares, and so we hauled them back. Once, while rambling through the draw, I caught sight of an unfamiliar bulge in the short grass. The coyotes had not yet disassembled the latest casualty, and I could see the red-brown hide flapping over the empty rib cage. I thought what a fine tipi I could make with the hide but could not bring myself to go any closer. The next time I wandered back, it was gone.

Just a few steps through the draw and across the wheat, lay the pasture. Every summer Dad turned a few head of cattle down the lane to graze there, along with the horses, which were glad to have a break from riding around the section. Since there was a pond in the pasture, they seldom came up the lane to the corral, so if I wanted to go riding, I had to walk down to bring them up. If they caught sight of the halter I was carrying, they took off, trotting easily away as soon as I got close. I learned to bring the grain bucket with me and hide the halter behind my back. The horses seemed resigned to their fate as we walked back to the corral, the cattle following docilely behind. If it became too hot to ride, they were turned back out, and I would unwillingly watch them gallop to freedom, tossing their heads, snorting and kicking.

The pasture was green only for a brief period during the spring when the rains filled the normally dry course that ran through it, and then on to Wild Horse Lake, until Dad dammed it up to make the stock pond. I wandered here as well, poking hopefully around for dinosaur bones in the old creek bed, and picking my way carefully amid the clumps of yellow-flowering prickly pear cactus, as well as the bristling soap weeds, their spines as sharp as the pins and needles Mom sewed with. I tried digging up the tiny, rounded cactus with the brilliant fuchsia flowers to plant by the house, but they always died.

The Farm on the Wall

It was still and quiet in the pasture, the only movements a glimpse of a pickup speeding down the road far off, leaving a plume of dust behind, or a hawk hovering over a jackrabbit frozen in a clump of grass. A slight depression in one corner was an old buffalo wallow, Dad said, and I would close my eyes and try to imagine how it looked without roads and telephone poles and scattered farms, filled instead with shaggy, brown bodies roaming to the horizon. Even here I found reminders of the past. The shallow furrows that traced across the pasture in meandering curves were left from Dust Bowl days, when Grandpa practiced contour farming to keep it from blowing away.

My science books described how to make an ant farm, so I walked down the lane that bordered the south side of the section and looked for red harvester ant hills. They weren't hard to find; all I had to do was look for the foot-high conical mounds underneath the barb-wire fence where they would be safe from my father's plow. The ants diligently scoured away all vegetation so that the ground was completely bare of buffalo grass and weeds for about three feet around each hill. The sides of the mound were covered with large grains of sand, all the same size. If the ants were in a field where Indians had chipped arrowheads and other tools, I would find tiny bits of flint as well. There might be two or three openings where I could watch the ants go in and out of the nest, returning with seeds and dead insects; if I looked carefully, I could see several of them walking along one of their trails, going out into the field to forage.

I didn't have two panes of glass to make the ant farm, but I figured one of Mom's canning jars would work just fine, after I punched some air holes in the top. I had to make sure I didn't make the holes too big, otherwise I would have a roomful of ants. I took the shovel from the wagon and plunged it into the side of the mound as hard as I could. Instantly, the ground was boiling with a red carpet of ants. I had taken care to slip on sneakers instead of the rubber flip-flops I normally wore, as the ants had a very painful bite that would last for days, but I danced around all the same, to shake off any that had starting climbing up my jeans.

Carol Winkler Kotsch

    Quickly, I dumped a shovelful of dirt and ants into the open Mason jar until it was full, screwed on the lid, put it in the wagon, and pulled it back home. Behind me the ants continued to mill around in a confused mass, but soon, they would start repairs, and in a few days, the nest would look the same as ever.

    My book recommended feeding the ants grape juice and sugar. I found that an aspirin lid worked well for the juice and scattered a small spoonful of sugar off to the side. The next day I discovered they had started making tunnels and I could watch them going up and down the insides of the jar. A queen was necessary to keep the farm going, but I couldn't tell if I had captured one or not. In a couple of weeks, the ants began to die off and I dumped the dirt out and looked around for something else.

    The fragrant flowers of the lilac bush attracted bees and butterflies, and Mom fashioned a butterfly net for me with netting and the rim of a plastic coffee can lid, though I was never very successful at catching any. Most of the butterflies were dull and drab skippers, as I discovered when I consulted my science books, but there were also brightly colored swallowtails and monarchs.

    I had the best luck with caterpillars. An empty coffee can worked well for a habitat and I took care to include the leaves they had been eating when I found them. The red and brown wooly-bears became lovely cream-colored moths with gold spots, but the most spectacular were the yellow, white, and black-banded caterpillars I found eating the carrot tops and the dill weed in the garden. When I touched one, a tiny, bright orange spine shot out, forked like a snake's tongue, and released a pungent stink.

    It was easy enough to put them into the coffee can, along with some carrot tops, and provide them with a stick or two to climb on. I punctured the plastic lid with some holes and checked on them daily. Within a week or so, they had made cocoons that were securely fastened to the twigs. I kept the lid off now and waited. One day, when I came home from school, I found a swallowtail butterfly fanning its drying wings on the wall of my bedroom. I showed it to my mother, and then I gently caught it and released it outside.

Ditches were riddled with small holes dug by thirteen-lined ground squirrels, where they, too, would be undisturbed from the tractor and plow. They popped up everywhere, but they were too fast for me to catch, although Dad did manage to snatch one. He brought it home one day, and I kept it in a wooden box. We didn't know what to feed it, but dry oatmeal seemed best. The ground squirrel, though, could not adjust to captivity and became dull and listless. I felt sorry for it and released it outside in the garden, and it quickly scurried away.

The larger holes in the sides of the ditches belonged to badgers. Dad warned us not to go poking around in one, since their jaws were strong enough to bite our hands off. I kept my distance, but badgers are nocturnal, and I never saw one, except once when I saddled up for a horseback ride before dawn. We occasionally glimpsed a skunk in the morning or evening, and knew well enough to leave it alone, especially if we saw one wandering around in daylight. *A daytime skunk is sick*, Dad said, *it probably has rabies. You run inside if you see one.* The tone of his voice told us this was serious.

Sometimes I spotted little prairie lizards as I wandered in the fields. They were small—only a few inches long—and matched the sandy soil so perfectly that I only noticed them as they dashed away, and then I glimpsed the bluish-green patch at their throat. Once, to my great surprise, I found a barred tiger salamander emerging from the drain in the basement under the shower; I recognized it right away from my *How and Why Wonder Book: Reptiles and Amphibians*, and wondered how it survived the baking heat without the puddles from the supply tank and the stock tank.

Great Plains toads were common enough around the farmhouse, especially if it had been a wet spring. Even if it had been dry, we could always count on finding tadpoles in the puddles next to the irrigation well up the hill where there would be standing water long enough for them to hatch. While Dad checked the motor on the well, and put in fresh oil, I scooped up handfuls of muddy, tadpole-filled water and poured them into a handy Mason jar. Back home, they would go into the old tubs from the washer that Grandma once used, and I watched every day as their tails disappeared and they gradually sprouted arms and legs. Finally, I turned them loose to hop away.

Uncle Lowell used to listen to them croak after a summer rain. They were really noisy, he said, but he never saw them during a dry spell, and wondered where they came from. After it rained, he and your grandpa would take off their shoes and turn up their pant legs and run in the mud.

Box turtles were also a fairly common sight crawling across the road or field. Dad would pick one up in the springtime, and I would keep it in a box. Every day I hunted under bricks and boards to find bugs and worms for it to eat, though they would eat baloney and dog food if I couldn't find enough. In the fall I turned them loose to find a place to spend the winter.

I prowled in and around the barn and the other buildings, and rambled down to the draw and pasture, but mostly I walked up and down the hill. That's how we always referred to it—just "up the hill," even though it was hardly more than a gentle swell across the otherwise featureless squares of farmland. When I stood at the top of the hill, I could look in every direction for miles and miles and watch the wheat rippling in a never-ending series of waves across the sections. In the spring it shimmered like green silk, and the rustling filled the silence.

I thought it was the most beautiful sight in the world, and I ran through the wheat, parting the stalks with my bare legs, arms outstretched and head tilted up. When I could run no more, I collapsed on my back to gaze breathless at the circle of blue above, framed with green and studded with snow-white clouds that drifted slowly out of my view. The green and the blue and the white are vivid beyond all else in my recollections. On the day before I left for college, I walked up the hill and looked for a long time at the view which was the most familiar thing in the world to me.

It was the highest hill in Gray County—2,820 feet above sea level. When Aunt Mae, O. R.'s daughter, was in her forties, Uncle Lowell told me she went to a fortune teller, who told her that her family had farmland and that oil would someday be flowing from the highest point. Various outfits test-drilled off and on while I was growing up, but the test holes always turned up dry.

A construction and survey crew from the National Geodetic Survey showed up at the hill one day in 1961 when I was just four years old. They were measuring the nation's topographical features, mapping elevations and distances for engineering and scientific purposes. Verifying boundaries was one outcome, but the maps would also be used by oil drillers looking for oil. They began building two towers, an inner tower where the surveying crew worked on a platform, and an outer tower they climbed to reach the inner one. I can just remember watching the crew gathered around their surveying instruments and leaning back to stare at the survey tower. It stood about 40 feet high and looked very much like Uncle's old windmill just a few yards away. Apart from the grain elevators in Montezuma and the surrounding small towns, it was the tallest thing I had ever seen. The survey marker they left is still there.

Dad climbed up there himself one night when he was cutting milo on the hill. The surveyors asked him to stop for a while; the lights on the combine were interfering with the signals they were flashing to other towers around the country in order to make measurements. He watched them work for a time, and when they were finished, he went back to cutting milo.

Sometimes Dad would pasture cattle on the grass up the hill, though not very many since it was not the best grazing land. After the cattle had cleaned it up, then it was time to roll up the barbwire and take down the fence posts. My brother and I tagged along to watch one day, and I tripped over the wire as it lay nearly hidden in the thin buffalo grass, and fell, hands outstretched, into a patch of prickly pear cactus. I remember frantically rolling around to escape the needles. Next, I am standing on the seat of the pickup, screaming and crying whenever Dad hit a bump and jostled me. And then I am standing naked on the kitchen table, with Dad on one side, tugging out the big needles with his pliers, and Mom on the other, plucking out the smaller ones with twee-

Carol Winkler Kotsch

zers.

A pit was cut into the side of the hill, a ground silo, where Dad stored the sorghum that was chopped into silage each fall. Bright green when it was dumped in, the sweet, juicy sorghum compacted as it settled and gave off a steady heat. It fermented all winter up the hill, turning brown as it aged. The cattle knew what was coming when they heard the tractor start up, and they jostled for position around the feed bunks, eagerly waiting for their share, and burying their noses deep into the feed as the tractor and feedcart passed by. The still-warm silage steamed in the cold winter air and gave off an unmistakable, rich, earthy, slightly alcoholic aroma, one I loved to inhale. Sometimes I held my hands over it to warm them. When the silage was gone, tumbleweeds rolled in to fill the silo instead, and I would burrow through them, creating tunnels and rooms to play in.

When Mom was tired of me hanging around the kitchen and getting in the way while she was fixing dinner, she would send me out to pick some flowers to make the table look pretty. I would walk up the hill, collecting flowers from the ditch as I went. Sunflowers, of course, though Mom objected to their strong aroma and sticky sap, but also the poppy mallow which I loved for its lovely deep magenta color—"wine cups" they were also called—and red and yellow Indian blanket flowers. I also picked some that I called shooting stars, though they weren't the same as that flower.

The bell-like flowers of the yucca were a beautiful creamy white, but the sharp spears that bristled around the base of the tall stalk where the flowers grew made it difficult for me to reach them. They were so sharp that early settlers called them Spanish bayonets. Down the hill, where water from the irrigation rows spilled over into the ditch, purple rushes grew, and an occasional strayed mallard duck floated by itself. There was usually a meadowlark sitting on a fencepost somewhere, trilling out its bubbling, flute-like call, a clear and beautiful song that always made me stop whatever I was doing so I wouldn't miss any of it. When I grew older, it seemed as though the wildflowers vanished, at least

The Farm on the Wall

in the ditches. They didn't appear to be missed by anybody but me.

My brother and I had a lemonade stand up the hill one summer. Mom let us mix a batch of Kool-Aid in a pitcher, and then helped us pack an old round coffee table into the trunk of the car, along with cups, and a box for our money, and hauled us up the hill. We sat on a couple of old milk crates waiting for business. The morning sun grew hotter and hotter, but farmers driving by were far and few between. Beefy was a loyal customer, but his daily nickels did not add up very fast, and we abandoned it after a few days.

I was fascinated by the mountains I saw in Colorado one year during a rare family vacation, and I wanted to go hunting for rocks like I had seen there. I had to be content instead with walking up and down the hill, poking through the gravel, instead of chipping at cliffs. It was hauled in from the sand pits by the Arkansas River next to Cimarron. Dad said we were lucky to have one so close; other counties didn't have a ready source and had to pay more to cover the miles and miles of roads that crisscrossed each county in neat squares. Mom sewed a rock-collecting bag for me from scraps of red velvet and Dad supplied a hammer welded from an old railroad spike to slip through the loop she had thoughtfully provided. I carried it up and down the hill, looking for new specimens to add to my collection.

I picked up anything that caught my eye and took it home and compared it to the pictures in my rock books. Quartz and granite were easy enough to identify, and jasper and flint, but other pieces mystified me; I could not tell if I had found shale or slate or limestone. The murky color pictures in my books were not much help. One day I picked up something very different. Blue-gray in color, it was three inches long, about the width of a pencil, and curved. I thought it was a fossil of some kind, but it didn't look like anything in my books. The next time we went to Dodge, Mom took me to the rock shop so I could show it to the owner. He was used to me coming in with a specimen that needed to be identified and told me that I had found a broken mastodon tooth, that had probably washed down the Arkansas River ages ago. Now I had another fossil to add to my collection. I loved to look around his shop at all the glittering crystals and gems and saved my allowance to purchase geodes and agates and crystals.

Close by to where Auntie and Uncle's house once stood, I found pieces of thick glass from old bottles that had turned purple after being in the sun so long, and bits of the good china, broken in some long-ago accident. The pattern of delicate flowers still showed as clearly as when Auntie had used them. There were also heavy chunks of old crockery lying about, dull and brown, once used to store pickles and sauerkraut. I picked them all up and tucked them away in my dresser where they rattled around until I cleared them out to make room for new treasures. I kept the marble I had found, though, convinced it was one my father had dropped and lost while playing up the hill with his brother and cousin Arlen.

When I was given a copy of Holling C. Holling's *Book of Indians*, I poured over his stories of the lives of Indian children of different tribes. It was best, I thought, to be like Rides-Away-Tinkling, who went galloping over the prairie on her mustang, the silver disks on her buckskin dress chiming as she rode. For the time being I had to be content with trotting along on Chief, but I could at least go hunting for arrowheads. There had been Indians around, Dad said, and he remembered Uncle finding arrowheads up on the hill.

I didn't really know how or where to look, but started walking over the fields by the house, and up and down the hill, my eyes glued to the ground. I found nothing but dirt and weeds and stubble. Then Fred Schmidt, the grownup son of Irvin and Rosie, our neighbors over to the southeast, dropped by. His family owned the land just east across the road from our hill where it continued on over to their section. Though it was a few feet lower than our hill, it still commanded a good view to the north. Irvin referred to it as "Arrowhead Hill" for all the arrowheads he and Fred had picked up there.

Fred had heard that I was interested in arrowheads and offered to take me on a hunt. He taught me where and how to look. *Keep your eyes open for little chips of waste flint*, he said, which would tell me that arrowheads had been made there. The tops of hills were best, I learned, as the Indians preferred to camp there in order to keep a look-out for approaching enemies or game. The perfect time to go hunting was right after a field had been plowed, and if the timing was right, rain had fallen afterwards. I usually went in the afternoon, right after dinner, so no shadows would obscure an arrowhead half buried in the sandy soil.

As I crisscrossed the top of Arrowhead Hill, I found knives for skinning hides; scrapers for cleaning off the flesh; tiny, delicate bird points; a lethal-looking spear point; a handful of pottery shards; and even a couple of beads, but I always picked up more pieces of discarded flint from making these tools than anything else. There was Alibates Flint from the Texas Panhandle that stood out with its gaudy stripes of pink, maroon, purple and orange, and delicate milky-white or crystal-clear chalcedony from South Dakota, but mostly I found the workday yellow-orange jasper from the Flint Hills or Smoky Hills here in Kansas. The piece of obsidian, a volcanic glass found by our neighbors, made a longer journey from Mexico, or the Yellowstone area, perhaps.

The Indians—the Kiowa-Apache—were typical Plains Indians who had been living in the Black Hills since the 1650's. From there they were pushed south by Cheyenne, Arapaho and Sioux tribes to the Platte River basin headwaters of the Arkansas, Cimarron, Canadian and Red Rivers.[1] The Comanche who were already living there resented these newcomers, and the two tribes battled for dominance, until 1790, when they made a pact to share the same hunting grounds.

The Kiowa were joined by Plains Apache, and along with the Comanche, they roamed and hunted bison across the southwestern plains. Wagon trains on the Santa Fe Trail began crisscrossing their territory in the 1820s, and settlers began pushing their way into the area in the 1840s, disturbing their hunting. The Kiowa-Apache and Comanche pushed back, even joining with former enemies to harass the traders and settlers.

Carol Winkler Kotsch

The government and military stepped in, establishing military posts and sending punitive expeditions. The Medicine Lodge Treaty of 1867 confined the Indians to reservations in southwestern Oklahoma, but very little of the promised food and supplies appeared, and the Kiowa-Apache and other tribes, facing starvation, continued raiding. As late as December 1872, a store in Pierceville, 20 miles west of Cimarron and on the railroad, was burned.[2] The government and military were relentless, however, during the Red River War, and in the end, the Indians were forced into submission and remained on their reservation.

I did find an arrowhead once, up on our hill. I had stepped right on it while jogging along the hill and across the road to Arrowhead Hill; Irvin had given me permission to hunt there anytime I liked. On my way back, I glanced down and saw a perfect red-gray flint point centered in a footprint I had made on the way over. Uncle must have found and collected most of the arrowheads up our hill, for I never found another one there, only a few pieces of flint. He kept his for years, but finally gave them away to a neighbor boy in Dodge City when he tired of having them clutter up his dresser.

Whenever I found something interesting, I would stand beside the mailbox the next day, waiting for Beefy to arrive with the morning mail and the latest goings-on in town. When he saw me, he knew I had found something and pretended mock dismay when he pulled up, especially if I had a big grin on my face, since that meant I had a perfect, unbroken point. He examined what I found with interest and showed me how to tell a scraper from a scrap of waste flint. Beefy liked to collect arrowheads himself, and sometimes he brought one of his points to show to me, but like other relic hunters, he kept his favorite hunting grounds a secret, so no one else could pick up something after him.

I hunted on sand hills northwest of the farm, and south by Crooked Creek, where I found my first perfect point. There were even a few traces left by the Indians on our farm as well, down the hill. Dad pulled out a heavy, misshapen stone ax from the foundations of the old farmhouse after it was moved in 1977. Later, when you girls were small, he bulldozed out the old shelter in the corral, just at the end of the haystack, there in the picture, and unknowingly uncovered a small cache of artifacts, scattering them behind the barn. Do you remember walking along with your father and me, and picking up some scrapers and hand axes, and a broken arrowhead? We even found a small piece of turquoise, too, that had come from somewhere in the Southwest.

I yearned to wander over to Wild Horse Lake as well, attracted by the stories I had heard Dad tell about the horse thief buried somewhere on the bluffs, and the arrowheads and ax heads neighbors had found there during the Dirty Thirties when the dust storms exposed artifacts that had been covered for decades. The sand hills that surrounded the lake had formed millions of years ago when the Arkansas River, about 15 miles off to the north, had carried sand and rocks down from the Rockies and deposited them as it slowed and meandered across the plain. Winds carried the sand off from the riverbanks and set it down in dunes miles away.

Beefy used to tell me that old-timers remembered seeing rings of stones on the sand hills beside the lake. He thought they might have been medicine wheels, sacred circles mainly found in the northern states and Canada for rituals and healing, but a state archaeologist for Kansas told me they were more than likely tipi rings, the stones being used to keep the edges of the tipi tight to the ground. They had long since been plowed under or picked up and tossed aside.

Though only two miles straight north of the farm, Wild Horse was too far away for Mom to holler for me, and she worried about the heavy grain trucks that rumbled down the road during harvest time. I had to wait until I could persuade Dad to drive me over, if he wasn't too tired in the evening, and could poke around in the sand hills with me. The creeping sand and buffalo grass had covered up the arrowheads again, however, and I found only a few pieces of flint and broken points. Later, when I was older, I rode my bike over, and later still, I drove the car.

A natural sinkhole, Wild Horse was edged by a bluff on the

west side that was perhaps twenty feet tall from the top down to the shoreline. It seemed very big to me, and I didn't know of anything larger until the first time we drove to Colorado for a vacation, and I saw how it was dwarfed by the foothills of the Rocky Mountains. The "bluff" was simply a large sand hill loosely held together by the sagebrush and cactus that grew everywhere. Someone, a church group I think Dad told me, had planted the row of elm trees at the top. They were stunted and gnarled compared to the well-watered elms I saw in Dodge City but had managed to survive. The cluster of sandy, lumpy hills that surrounded Wild Horse looked very different from the smoothly plowed fields by the farm, and indeed, the yucca-covered dunes were no good for planting wheat or milo. The farmer who owned the land kept cattle pastured there, which I thought added to its untamed appearance.

Run-off from thunderstorms kept it filled, though it shrank or expanded depending on the weather. Dad pointed out the old highwater mark where the soap weeds stopped growing. Wild mustangs used to go there for water, Dad said, and the early settlers managed to capture some to break as workhorses. He didn't know any details about the horse thief or exactly where he was supposed to be buried. I always kept an eye out for a likely looking gravesite, but his executioners had not seen fit to mark it.

As farmers leveled out their fields for irrigation, and dammed off the small creeks that drained into the lake, it began to dry up, but during the sixties there was still enough water for the locals to go water-skiing, though only one or two boats at a time. It was a place for picnics on Sunday afternoons, and I spotted fishing poles sticking out of the sandy shoreline. At night, teenagers would drive down to the lake, with the headlights on their cars turned off, for illicit beer parties. Years later when I walked across the dry lakebed, I found crumbling snail shells and old Coke bottles and rusting beer cans.

I carefully arranged the arrowheads I had found in a starburst pattern inside a shadow box and hung it on the walls of my room. From time to time I would take it down to add a new find or arrange it into a different pattern. I discarded many things I grew up with—stuffed animals, toys, dolls, posters, beads—but the arrowheads always remained. They came with me after your father and I married, and now hang next to the farm on the wall, a link to the people who were there before my family, and of the time I spent there, walking through the fields and up the hill, and exploring around the barn and corral.

18

Off to School by Horse and Bus

In the late afternoons or early evening, when the shadows were long, I would hop up in the pickup with Dad and go with him to check wells in the summer, or count cattle and break ice in the winter. We were about a mile north of Wild Horse one evening, when I spotted a stucco-covered building with boarded-up windows; a couple of plows were parked right next to the walls. Tall weeds grew around it. It looked very lonesome. *Who lives there?* I asked. *Nobody does*, Dad told me. *It's not a house—it's an old one-room school, North Lone Star.* He paused and added, *I used to go to one myself until I was in the fifth grade.*

    I was incredulous once more at this bit of news. It was hard to believe that my father had attended a one-room schoolhouse; that was something from out of the remote past, from the days of the pioneers. But one-room schools were, in fact, scattered all over the Montezuma Township, indeed, all over Kansas. A couple of sections might support up to four or eight farm families, each with several children. The neighbors would form a district about

Carol Winkler Kotsch

two miles in each direction, with the school to be located on a bit of donated ground somewhere close to the center.[1]

Dad and Uncle Lowell both attended one a mile west and a mile south of the farm for several years. Homestead School, it was called, incorporated by local homesteader farmers. It had been built in 1909 at a cost of $1500, Dad remembered. At first, there was no well and water had to be carried from a nearby farm, but a windmill was added later.[2] There was a shelter for the horses the students rode to school, and a shed to store coal for the stove. The students had to make do with two outhouses in back, unlike North Lone Star, which had indoor chemical toilets. Dad and the other Homestead students were envious, especially in the wintertime. A solitary tree in back provided a little shade at recess. Each August, a local farmer would bring in a horse-drawn mower to cut down the nearly-shoulder high weeds so the children could play.

Uncle began serving on the school board in 1924, and Grandpa in 1929 and both remained on the board until 1941. When Uncle Lowell began first grade in 1932, his mother made a special outfit for him to wear on the first day, but the virtuous Mennonite children, dressed in their severe plainclothes, teased him about the knickers and jacket and tie that were fashionable for the day. He looks very dapper in the photo of his class, but in next year's picture, he is wearing overalls.

There were seven rows of desks in the classroom, Uncle Lowell remembered, with the youngest class sitting in the smallest desks at the front, and the older children in the largest desks at the back of the room, about 32 students all together. The teacher, who was sometimes barely older than her students, would call them up a grade at a time to listen to them recite and then send them back to their desks while she worked with the next class. Soon the small room filled with whispers and rustlings as each row began to practice the day's lesson, growing louder and louder until the teacher had to call them to attention.

During the early days of one-room schoolhouses, the teachers would be unevenly educated themselves, but gradually, certified teachers began arriving from Emporia with a newly-earned degree in primary or secondary education, and then later from Pittsburg or Hays. Men were preferred, but during World War I when there was a shortage of men, schools began hiring female teachers. After the war, when better jobs for men became available in business and industry, women dominated in schools so they would not compete with men elsewhere.[3]

In the wintertime, the teacher would arrive an hour early to fill the stove with coal, and start a fire so the room would be warm when the students arrived, but sometimes they had to keep their coats on and put their bottles of frozen ink around the stove to thaw before class could start. Local families took turns boarding the teachers who were paid $20 a month, plus an extra $5 if they cleaned the building. The Winkler family boarded the last teacher, Dad recalled, who spent half the year with them.

When Uncle Lowell started third grade, he had a horse to ride, Babe, bought from a local man who could no longer feed her. Some oats and good pasture filled out the skin and bones, and Uncle Lowell found out that as soon as his foot touched the stirrup, she was gone. One day, at the end of school, as he was hoisting himself into the saddle for the ride home, Babe unexpectedly took off, brushing against some lumber blocking the stall door and ripping off a stirrup. Uncle Lowell lost his balance, turned loose and rolled off, while Babe headed home at a dead run without him.

When the riderless pony showed up, Grandma and Grandpa rushed off in the farm truck, fearing they would find Lowell lying injured on the road. He was bruised and shaken, but mounted Babe the next morning for another ride to school.

Three years later, when his younger cousin Arlen started school, Grandpa and Uncle turned an old four-wheel buggy into a two-wheel pony cart, and produced an old slow horse named Jack who was trained to pull a cart. Now Uncle Lowell rode to the top of the hill to pick up Arlen for the trip to school. It was a slower ride, and cold during the winter in the open cart, but they wrapped up in blankets to keep warm.

When Dad was old enough, he joined them in the cart. Neigh-

Carol Winkler Kotsch

bor Susie Giesbrecht remembered "Lowell and Riley Winkler coming to school in their horse and buggy, cute little sister sitting between. Was a pretty picture."[4] Susie had probably confused Arlen for her younger cousin, Shirley.

Though Grandpa and Uncle fed the horses well, they developed what was called "blind staggers," swaying and stumbling when they walked. Soon they went blind, and their legs could no longer support them. It was likely due to eating milk vetch, or locoweed, as it was more commonly known. I can remember a small patch of it up the hill. I thought the purple flowers were pretty, but knew better than to pick any. Both horses were dead within the year, and Dad walked from first grade to fourth grade, though on cold days his father would drive him.

When my father started school, he wore bib overalls and shirts picked out from the mail-order catalog. Soon he discovered that he was mistaken for a Mennonite boy, and asked his mother for pants and a belt when the overalls wore out. There were new shoes in the fall from the Sears store in Dodge City, which he had to carefully clean after milking the cows at night in order to wear them the next day. At the little mercantile store in Montezuma, Grandma might let him pick out a pencil with the multiplication table printed on it.

For his first three years, he and Lowell carried their lunches to school, hard-boiled eggs, or a meatloaf or egg salad sandwich, along with an apple. In 1941, his final year at the school when he was in fourth grade, hot lunches became available for a penny a day. A couple of farmers' wives would prepare lunch from government surplus—canned beef, salt pork, dry beans, cans and boxes of fruit—at their homes, and deliver it to the school, Dad remembered. Ham and bean soup, and carrots were frequent, but it was hot and fresh, and seemed like a luxury to him.

It was also that same year that Homestead received some playground equipment—a cast iron merry-go-round that made the students feel they were now on a par with the town kids at recess time. Now they had something to play on after their games of baseball, fox and geese, and handy over, Dad's favorite.

Two teams were chosen and stood on opposite sides of the schoolhouse. When the team without the ball yelled out "handy over," the other side flung the ball over the roof of the school. After one of the players caught the ball, he would follow the rest of his team as they rushed around both sides of the schoolhouse and use it to tag as many of the rival team as possible. His teammates would act as if they were carrying a ball themselves in order to confuse the other side. Players who had been tagged then became members of the team that caught them, and when everyone was caught, the game began again.[5]

There were over 7000 one-room schools in Kansas from 1928 to 1945, but as farms decreased and towns and cities grew, districts began to consolidate for the savings, and better educational opportunies.[6] In Montezuma, consolidation began in 1941, and all the one-room schools scattered about the district--Owl, Eagle, Fry, South Lone Star, Big Blue, South Salem, North Gray, Haggard, Sod College, Sunnyside, Gray Center, Pleasant Ridge, Diamond, Center View, and Richland—were closed.

At Homestead, when teacher James Shepherd took another job at a higher salary closer to his home in early September, the school board had no chance to hire another one at such short notice, and the school board voted to consolidate with Montezuma. The little school was closed on September 19 and auctioned off on the 30th. Besides the building itself, bidders could make offers for the coal stove, three tons of coal, one piano, a barn, a coalhouse, two toilets, one telephone, and stock in the telephone line. Homestead was moved to Garden City and used as a church for a time. For years afterwards Dad could still find it when the family traveled to Garden City to visit Grandma's youngest sister Ruth, who had married and joined the rest of the family in western Kansas. Other empty schoolhouses were used for storage by nearby farmers.

The new consolidated grade school had nine teachers and 222 students, about half of whom lived out in the country. It was just about a block west of the high school, which had been built and accredited in 1916; the first graduating class was in 1918. Dad and

Carol Winkler Kotsch

Uncle Lowell rode one of the four new busses to their first day in the new school. When Dad got off the bus and made his way inside the new building, he was startled to discover that his fifth grade class had 29 other students, instead of only four or five, children his own age who lived perhaps only a few miles away, but ones he had never met before. It took a little time to learn so many new names, but at recess he could still play on the merry-go-round that had been transferred from Homestead. When I started school, I played on it as well, unaware that it dated to my father's time. The wooden seats had been replaced, but the cast-iron frame remained as sturdy as ever. It was still there when you girls and your Grandpa and I posed for a picture on it in 1993, but time caught up with it at last, and it was removed not long after.

When I started school, I attended the first kindergarten class ever offered in Montezuma. It lasted only six weeks but was not welcomed by everyone in town as it meant the expense of another teacher. Dad had been elected to the school board at about the time I began in 1962 and remembered that they worked with St. Mary's of the Plains in Dodge City to bring out the kindergarten teacher.

Going to kindergarten and seeing other children my own age must have been a big change from my days of solitary play with my brother on the farm, as it had been for my father, but it did not seem to make a big impression on me. I can only remember a few things—bouncing a ball back and forth with another child, coloring a picture of a smiling sun, and being permitted to look at a book. My brother did not understand what was happening when the bus picked me in the morning and fussed about my absence until he and Mom picked me up at noontime.

In first grade I carried a pencil, scissors, crayons, a Big Chief tablet, and a little braided rest mat to school. Now my brother and I rode the bus together in the morning, though Mom still had to make the trip to town at noon to pick him up after kindergarten, which had been extended for the entire year. I recognized two other students: one of the Love boys from the farm west of us, and Beefy and Genie's youngest son, with whom my brother and I sometimes played when Dad and Mom went to town.

The rest of the children were unknown to me, and nearly all of them were Mennonites. The girls wore long, plain-colored dresses, and had their hair in braids. They did not watch TV or read the Sunday funnies, or listen to the radio, and like their parents had done for my father and uncle, my Mennonite classmates were quick to let me know when my soul was in peril, solemnly assuring me that wearing the genuine plastic ruby ring from my Christmas dress-up set would cause me to burn in hellfire. They seemed to reject everything I enjoyed doing, and their self-righteous attitudes were grating, but they were the only girls to play with until about the third grade when a new family moved to town with school-age daughters.

Mrs. Monniger, who had taught Uncle Lowell in first grade, was now in charge of the school cafeteria. She oversaw the other ladies in the lunchroom, Mennonite women who were masters at preparing simple and filling food. They had to be creative with what they could afford to buy, and any government surplus commodities they received. We were encouraged to clean up everything on our plates, but I could not eat the cooked spinach; it was slimy and had a strong taste that made me gag.

Midmorning on cold winter days, I could sometimes smell the combined perfume of chili and cinnamon rolls drifting down the halls from the kitchen, and I would give a happy sigh; they were always prepared together. Beans were one of the surplus staples distributed by the state, and they were served to us as chili or ham and beans. Chili was still a somewhat unfamiliar food, and to entice us to eat it, the cooks would make cinnamon rolls by hand to go with it.[7] The seasonings may not have been authentic, but it was still good nonetheless; I don't remember seeing much go to waste.

Raisins were another commodity, and were turned into raisin pie, a Mennonite recipe commonly made for funerals as it kept well and did not need refrigeration. The crust was thick like a cobbler and sprinkled with sugar. It was not so popular with my classmates, and I was able to eat all the raisin pie I wanted on those days.

At recess time, I played with my own jump rope, or helped turn a big rope as skippers jumped in and out to our chants. I can remember "Mother May I" and "Red Rover," and we played crack the whip and tag when we were tired of the swings and monkey bars and the merry-go-round. I received roller skates for Christmas and brought them to school along with my skate key and skated up and down the sidewalks in front of the building. The only time I could use my skates was during the school year; there were no sidewalks on the farm, of course, and our hand-poured basement floor was too bumpy and small.

The grade school in Montezuma was too big to play handy over as my father had done, but we would all join in to play "Black Man." Lining up against the wall of the bus garage, we would dash across an open space to the school wall opposite. The last one across was it. Now we darted back and forth from the garage wall to the school wall, while the person who was it tried to tag us. If we were caught, then we were it as well, and joined in tagging the rest of the children, until everyone was caught, and we started over.

It was time for a rest after recess. We placed our mats next to our desks and lay down in obedient silence while Mrs. Hargett graded papers. Sometimes one of my classmates would fall asleep, but I found it hard to remain still, and picked at the scabs on my knees I had gotten from falling down while skating. After fifteen or so minutes, we got up and resumed our learning.

In Mrs. Hargett's first grade classroom I learned to add and subtract, and to read. Numbers were troubling to me. Addition was straightforward enough, but subtraction eluded me for some time. I used fingers and counted and wrote and erased so many times I wore holes in my worksheet. The rest of the class seemed unfazed by it and wondered at my slowness. I would struggle with math all through school, puzzling my mother, who had saved her high school math books and worked trigonometry problems for fun. She would help me at night, but the numbers perversely re-

The Farm on the Wall

fused to make sense. I gritted my teeth and tried again, and felt tears beginning as I tried to solve another problem.

Learning to read was different. Each day Mrs. Hargett would write a new word on the blackboard—I especially remember "violet," a lovely, graceful word, I thought, and said it over and over to myself. Using blunt-nosed scissors we cut out innumerable rectangles containing words that had to be matched and arranged in the appropriate location on the worksheet. The lid to my paste jar had a brush attached to it, and I would swipe it across the slip of paper and smooth it down into the correct column. It was laughably easy to me, though very tedious and messy, and I, in my turn, could not understand why some of my classmates found it hard.

Mom listened to me practice, correcting my mispronunciations, and soon I was breezing along, reading out loud from Dick and Jane without hesitation. It was dreary listening to my classmates as they stumbled over words, reading in a monotone, making sentences run together without pause or expression. During the bus ride, I would ask to borrow readers from older students and would pour through a chapter or two before the bus pulled up in front of school.

The school did not have a library until I was in the third grade, but each classroom had a small shelf of books that could be checked out. I caught sight of a brand-new book one day on that shelf. The front cover was a vivid orange and green with a yellow duckling on it. I asked Mrs. Hargett to let me check it out, but it was too close to the bell. I would have to wait until Monday. I thought about that book all weekend, but on Monday when I returned to school, someone else got to it before I did, and I had to wait again.

One day—I remember it was cool and rainy—Mom announced she was going to take me to the library in Montezuma. I had no idea there was a library in town and wasn't too sure what one was. It was very quiet and empty when we walked in, but right away I noticed the smell of paper and ink, a smell peculiar to each library I've been in since. I didn't know where to start, but eventually found the animal books by Thornton Burgess. I was en-

Carol Winkler Kotsch

chanted with his stories of Grandfather Frog, Old Mr. Toad, Jimmy Skunk, Buster Bear, Old Mother West Wind, the Merry Little Breezes, the Smiling Pool, Paddy the Beaver, and Little Joe Otter.

The librarian, Mrs. Boyd, permitted only two books to be checked out at a time, on Monday, Wednesday, and Saturday afternoons from 1 to 5. I made my way through all of the Burgess books, and then started on Nancy Drew, the Hardy Boys, and the Black Stallion series. If I finished my books before our next trip to town—and I always did—I re-read them or pawed through the bookshelves in the living room for something else to read.

Mom and Dad had belonged to a book of the month club years before, and the shelves were full of forgotten best-sellers, *Reader's Digest* condensed books and a faux leather-bound series of the classics. There was also a copy of *Alice in Wonderland*. It had pictures and color plates and seemed to be written for children. It was much bigger and harder than anything else I had read, but I started in on it.

I was alternately fascinated and repelled by it but could not stop reading it. The picture of Bill the Lizard was very scary to me, but I loved the color plate of the playing cards painting the roses in the Queen of Heart's garden, so much that I tore it out. I would re-read it many times—always skipping past Bill—but it was never a comfortable book for me.

Sometimes I would find stories I could read in the Reader's Digest books—it helped that they were condensed—and in this way I was exposed to many great titles and authors. *A Christmas Carol* was one of them, and I started looking for similar titles. I picked up my mother's copy of *Hawaii*, a thick best-seller of the 1960s, and began plowing through it as a sixth-grader. When I finished, I tossed it aside and went back to the Hardy Boys for a time.

Now all I wanted for Christmas and my birthday was books, which concerned my relatives; surely, I wanted something else more interesting and suitable for a girl. Mom finally convinced them otherwise, and soon my small shelves were full, and my collection spilled over to my dresser. When it was too hot to go outside, I spent every moment curled up on my bed reading, and Mom would have to drag me out to help in the kitchen and remind me to go water the chickens and check on my calves. When I reached high school and was old enough to drive, I went to work at the library for Mrs. Boyd, processing the new books, checking them out, and shelving them. Sometimes I would find my name written from years before on the checkout cards and I would reread my favorite stories.

Like Francie in *A Tree Grows in Brooklyn*, "my school days went along. Some were made up of meanness...others were bright and beautiful..." As I went from grade to grade, from kindergarten to high school, I learned much of the same things my father had in the generation before, and you girls in the generation after; reading, writing, math, science, history, English, and geography. We all sang and played instruments and gave Christmas concerts for parents. We ran laps in gym and played at recess. The technology was different for each generation—Dad and Uncle Lowell learned to type on manual typewriters; I had electric typewriters and adding machines, and you girls used computers and calculators. It was not easy to attract teachers to southwest Kansas, but we had a few good ones, and from them my father and uncle and I received an education sound enough to send us on our way.

19

The Generations After

After I left the farm for college, and then married your father, and we started our family, I found myself picking up after my relatives, just as I had once picked up after the Indians. I saved the things that told the most about them. Mom's old riding boots stand in a corner, and the jewel-tone velvet quilt she stitched drapes the stair railing. The table runner on the back of David Graves' rocking chair was crocheted by Mary Winkler, and Grammie's old glass canning jar holds wheat from a long-ago harvest. The framed handkerchief was hand-embroidered by Arria Etherton Graves. I have Grammie's recipes for fudge and whole-wheat sour cream muffins in my recipe box and think of her when I make them. Once, O.R. offered candy to grandchildren and visitors from a cut-glass dish; now it is filled with salt and sits on my kitchen counter. Like the clocks and washstand, these objects are similar to the fossils I once collected; I pick them up and examine them and remember the stories of their owners.

Perhaps someday someone will walk where I did, and notice traces my family left behind—nails and bolts, porcelain insulators for stringing fence, a wrench dropped while making repairs, a cast-off horseshoe, a forgotten, unrecognizable toy, or the patch of rhubarb. I used to look for the old patch of rhubarb up the hill myself every year; even after I went off to college, I would walk up the hill to poke around in the weeds until I found it. Mom and Dad had planted it there many years ago next to the windmill when they first married, and it grew faithfully for years and years after they moved down the hill. I would stand there and think of my mother, and Grammie and Auntie, and all the hard labors these women had performed while they lived on the farm.

The patch up the hill died out eventually, but the patch down the hill lived on when Mom and Dad built their new farmhouse halfway up the hill, and Mom transplanted some to a new garden. She continued to make rhubarb pies from it, though not as many, as I wasn't around to eat them. Every time your father and I and you girls went out to visit, I would pick some to take home and make into pie myself. I tried transplanting some of the roots to our home in Wichita, but it never took to the foreign soil.

The patch Mom transplanted halfway up the hill will also come up faithfully every spring for years and years, though no one will look at it and remember the men and women I knew who lived there and labored to run a farm and raise a family. Someday, it too, will die off, and the land will change and all the things I knew and loved on the farm, and up the hill will be gone. The boots will be tossed out, the quilt will fall to pieces, the canning jar will shatter, and the arrowheads will lose their meaning. Even the unchanging farm on the wall may someday become lost in the shuffle of years.

When my grandpa finished telling me the bare bones of O. R.'s life all those years ago, I was awestruck by the story and could not wait to tell Dad what I had found out. Dad smiled patiently as I excitedly poured out Grandpa's account; he had heard it many times himself. I didn't forget O. R.'s story, but with the self-centeredness of a teenager, I didn't ask Grandpa again for more family history. How I wish I had; so many pieces are missing. I've filled them in as best I can and hope I've come close. "Some facts may be fuzzy and untrue," Evalina Field Gasswint wrote, "but can be real and until we have better understanding, we will suppose

The Farm on the Wall

they are true." Like Evalina, I beg forgiveness for facts I have incorrectly recorded.

Our histories—our stories—that we choose to remember and tell, shape us as much as we shape them in the retelling. As I listened to my dad and his brother, my grandpa and grandma, I heard of O. R.'s journey, my grandparents' struggles with drought, and my father's childhood, and later, I learned about my mother's mining background. All these accounts once amused me, and taught me, giving me a sense of identity and belonging. I gained a connection to people and places I had never met or seen and learned to make some sense of the world and its challenges. I came to understand that it rained on the just and the unjust alike, and that nature could be uncaring, and that sometimes there was nothing else for it but to carry on and make do with what you had.

My great-grandfather's story is a common enough account of an ordinary man, similar to millions of others. Many times growing up, and as an adult, I would ask myself—could I have done what O. R. did? Could I have left all that was familiar, and gone on a long and hazardous journey by myself at that age, with no guarantee of success when it was over? But that's what life is, after all, and I remembered that story during difficult times and persevered. It became an orientation point for me; after I moved away from the farm and was taken up with a family and other interests, I returned to it again and again, always trying to find out more.

And did O. R.'s story have a successful ending? You will have to decide for yourselves, but I rather think it did. He did not become a wealthy man or do anything noteworthy to the rest of the world, but from his chaotic early life, he created stability with Mary and their children, and laid the foundations for future prosperity; a fine legacy for any family. My challenges—and yours, girls—are different from O. R.'s, but nonetheless demanding. So it is for each generation.

I look at the farm on the wall and think about my great-grandfather, and recall all the stories I heard; I remember the horses and cattle and pets, my own wanderings under the hot summer sun and cold winter wind, the patch of rhubarb, and the fields of waving wheat, and it all lives again. The people in the stories are

Carol Winkler Kotsch

mostly gone now, and I have only a few belongings to remember them by. The stories they left me, though, are not like the fossils I once collected, frozen and fixed in time. They are also your stories, to continue for yourselves, to change and correct, and to hand on in your turn. And as long as that happens, they will continue to live and outlast the farm on the wall, and shape future generations.

My childhood's home I see again,
And sadden with the view;
And still, as memory crowds my brain,
There's pleasure in it too.
O Memory! thou midway world
'Twixt earth and paradise,
Where things decayed and loved ones lost
In dreamy shadows rise,
And, freed from all that's earthly vile,
Seem hallowed, pure, and bright,
Like scenes in some enchanted isle
All bathed in liquid light.

Abraham Lincoln
1846

Sources

Chapter 2: Land Boom in the Great American Desert

1. Bradsher, Greg. "How the West Was Settled" *Prologue*, Winter, 2012, p. 28.

2. *Kansas: A Guide to the Sunflower State Federal Writers Project. Tour 4A and 4B*. New York: Hastings House 1939, p 398-400. (New York: Hastings House, 1939), 398-400.

3. Ibid.

4. Rennie, Helen Ward. *Tale of Two Towns*. Dallas: Royal Publishing Company, 1961, p. 36.

5. "The Commonwealth" July 30, 1886 Gray County Clippings, v.1, 1885-1981, Kansas State Historical Society, K978.1 G79, p.3.

6. Ibid.

7. Arkansas Valley Sanitarium Association. *The New West Sanitarium*. n.p.: n.d. (K/978.1/-G79/Pam.v.1/no. 4). Kansas State Historical Society.

8. *The Barton County Democrat*, Great Bend December 4, 1890, p. 4.

9. Camilla Cave Collection, Kansas Collection, RH MS 598, Kenneth Spencer Research Library, University of Kansas Libraries. Box 15 folder 19 "Lester Luther: History of parents and family, 1955" p. 2.

10. Ibid.

11. Ibid, p. 3.

12. Luther, F.M., and sons. "Two Stories." 1911. TS. C338 .109781 F679tw Western History (Conservation, Tenth Mountain Division) Collection, The Denver Public Library.

13. "*The Travail of Cimarron and Ingalls and the Death of Montezuma*" Excerpted from "*Collections of the Kansas State Historic Society, 1911-1912*", edited by George W. Martin, Secretary. Vol XII., State Printing Office, Topeka, Kansas, 1912, p463-467.

14. "Mr. Soule's Winning Gamble," *Discovering America's Past: Customs,*

Legends, History and Lore of Our Great Nation, Pleasantville, New York: Readers Digest, 1993 p 27.

15. *"The Travail of Cimarron and Ingalls and the death of Montezuma"*, p463-467.

16. Dallin, Dorothy. *"'Phantom' Railroad Caused Great Strife." The Topeka Daily Capital*, May 1, 1932. p. 6B.

17. Miner, H. Craig. *West of Wichita: Settling the High Plains of Kansas.* Lawrence Ks: University of Kansas Press, 1986, p. 183.

18. Schellenberg, James A. *Conflict between Communities: American County Seat Wars.* New York: Paragon House Publishers, 1987 "Shootout at Cimarron" p 16-20.

19. *Early Montezuma, West of Wichita, Travail of Cimarron*

20. *"'Phantom' Railroad Caused Great Strife*, p. 6B.

21. Williams, Walter. "The Parting of the Ways: An Old Santa Fe Trail." *The Wichita Beacon*, September 9, 1911, p. 16.

22. Schellenberg, James A. Conflict between Communities: American County Seat Wars. "Shootout at Cimarron." New York: Paragon House Publishers, 1987, p. 16-20.

23. Ibid.

24. Basye, Ruby. *"Bloody battle with Four Dead Climax of Gray County Feud between Cimarron, Ingalls." Wichita Eagle Magazine*, March 11, 1956.

25. *The Osage City Free Press*, Osage City, Ks, Mar 21, 1889, p. 4.

26. *"Once upon a time in America,"* by Tony Storey, The Sole Society http://www.sole.org.uk//onceupon.htm, 3/22/2008.

27. *Semi-weekly interior journal.* (Stanford, Ky.), 21 Jan. 1890. *Chronicling America: Historic American Newspapers.* Lib. of Congress. <http://chroniclingamerica.loc.gov/lccn/sn85052020/1890-01-21/ed-1/seq-2/> 10/15/2015.

28. *Kansas: A Guide to the Sunflower State Federal Writers Project.* "Tour 4A and 4B," New York: Hastings House, 1939, p 398-400.

29. Greer, Bob. "Up from the depths: a Major historic find." *The Cimarron Jacksonian*, December 21, 1977.

30. *"Once upon a time in America,"* by Tony Storey, The Sole Society. http://www.sole.org.uk//onceupon.htm, 3/22/2008.

31. Miner, H. Craig. *West of Wichita: Settling the High Plains of Kansas*. Lawrence Ks: University of Kansas Press, 1986 p. 182.

32. *Kansas: A Guide to the Sunflower State Federal Writers Project*. "Tour 4A and 4B" New York: Hastings House 1939. p 398-400.

33. Camilla Cave Collection, Kansas Collection, RH MS 598, Kenneth Spencer Research Library, University of Kansas Libraries. Box 15 folder 19 "Lester Luther: History of parents and family, 1955" p. 12.

34. *Tale of Two Towns*, p. 63.

35. Rennie, Helen Ward. "Early Montezuma 1886-1895." *Cimarron Jacksonian*, Feb 16, 1961. Gray County Clippings, 978.1 G79 Clip V1, p121. Kansas State Historical Society.

36. Dallin, Dorothy. "'Phantom' Railroad Caused Great Strife." *The Topeka Daily Capital*, May 1, 1932, p. 6B.

37. *The Gray Book*. No pub date. Designed and printed by *The Jacksonian*, Cimarron, Kansas.

38. Yancey, Diane. *Life during the Dust Bowl*. San Diego: Lucent Books, 2004 p. 19.

39. *Water and the Making of Kansas* by Victoria Foth, Kansas Natural Resource Council, 1988 and 2010 http://www.knrc.ws/watermk09.htm 8/13/2008.

40. Miner, H. Craig. *Next Year Country: Dust to Dust in Western Kansas, 1890-1940*. Lawrence KS: University of Kansas Press, 2006, p. 40.

41. "Grading the Santa Fe," *The Liberal Democrat*, Feb 16, 1912, p. 1.

42. Rennie, Helen Ward. "Early Montezuma 1886-1895." *Cimarron Jacksonian*, Feb 16, 1961. Gray County Clippings, 978.1 G79 Clip V1, p121. Kansas State Historical Society.

43. Camilla Cave Collection, Kansas Collection, RH MS 598, Kenneth Spencer

Research Library, University of Kansas Libraries. Box 15 folder 19 "Lester Luther: History of parents and family, 1955" p. 9.

44. Camilla Cave Collection, Kansas Collection, RH MS 598, Kenneth Spencer Research Library, University of Kansas Libraries. Box 15 folder 19 "Lester Luther: History of parents and family, 1955" p. 10.

45. Luther, F.M., and sons. "Two Stories." 1911. TS. C338 .109781 F679tw Western History (Conservation, Tenth Mountain Division) Collection, The Denver Public Library.

46. An email Tuesday, March 31, 2015 9:46 AM, Patty Nicholas <pnichola@fhsu.edu> University Archivist/ Special Collections at Fort Hays State University; information from Leo Oliva, author, and Santa Fe Trail historian.

47. "Local News," *The Jacksonian* (Cimarron, KS), August 25, 1910, p. 6.

Chapter 3: Taking a Gamble

1. "Golden Jubilee of Mr. and Mrs. Winkler." *The Daily News*, Lockport Department, Joliet, Illinois, 12/4/1909, p. 10.

2. "Thuringia." https://en.wikipedia.org/wiki/Thuringia last updated April 27, 2016.

3. "Passenger Departure Lists of German Emigrants, 1709-1914," by Friedrich R. Wollmershäuser, 1997 www.progenealogists.com/germany/articles/gdepart.htm. 9/2092013.

4. Daniels, Roger, ed. *Coming to America*, 2nd ed. New York: Perennial, 2002, p. 146.

5. "Emigrant Trains: Migratory Transportation Networks Through Germany and the United States 1847-1914," by Nicole Ingrid Kvale; a dissertation submitted in partial fulfillment of the requirements for the degree of Doctor of Philosophy (History) at the University of Wisconsin, Madison, 2009 http://www.docstoc.com/docs/47513458/Emigrant-trains-Migratory-transportation-networks-through-Germany-and-the-United-States-1847--1914/ p. 11.

6. "Passenger Departure Lists of German Emigrants, 1709-1914," by Friedrich R. Wollmershäuser, 1997 www.progenealogists.com/germany/articles/gdepart.htm, 9/20/2013.

7. Tannahill, Reay. *Food in History*. New York: Stein and Day, 1973 p. 353.

8. Alexander, June. Daily Life in Immigrant America, 1870-1920: *How the Second Great Wave of Immigrants Made Their Way in America*. Chicago: Ivan R. Dee, 2009 p. 36.

9. *Daily Life in Immigrant America*, p. 36;

10. Hillstrom, Kevin. *Dream of America: 1870-1920*. Detroit, Michigan: Omnigraphics, 2009, p 37.

11. *Dream of America*, p. 38;

12. *Daily Life in Immigrant America*, p. 38;

13. *Dream of America*, p. 36;

14. Powell, John. *Encyclopedia of North American Immigration*. New York: Fact on File, 2005 p390;

15. Novotny, Ann. *Strangers at the Door: Ellis Island, Castle Garden and the Great Migration to America*. Riverside, Connecticut: Riverside Press, 1971, p. 51.

16. *Dream of America*, p 41.

17. http://www.yonderplaces.com/orphantrains/14_castlegarden.htm; Yonder Places Ancestry Magazine, March/April, 2003, v. 21, n. 2 "Castle Garden, the forgotten Gateway" by Barry Moreno; 9/22/2013

18. *Strangers at the Door*. p.44.

19. *Dream of America*, p. 45.

20. "Castle Garden-America's First Official Immigration Center," by Kimberly Powell http://genealogy.about.com/od/ports/p/castle_garden.htm 7/17/2008

21. *Strangers at the Door*, p. 53.

22. http://www.yonderplaces.com/orphantrains/14_castlegarden.htm; Yonder Places Ancestry Magazine, March/April, 2003, v. 21, n. 2 "Castle Garden, the forgotten Gateway" by Barry Moreno; 9/22/2013

23. "Castle Clinton National Monument "National Park Service, http://genealogy.about.com/gi/o.htm?zi=1/XJ&zTi=1&sdn=genealogy&cdn=parenting&tm=611&f=10&su=p284.13.342.ip_p504.6.342.ip_&tt=11&bt=1&bts=1&zu=http%3A//www.nps.gov/cacl/ 10/20/2008

24. *Little Falls Herald*. Friday, September 1, 1905, p. 2.

25. "O.R. Winkler passes away Sunday." *The Montezuma Press*, March 20, 1941, v. 28, p. 1.

26. University of Illinois Archives University of Illinois at Urbana-Champaign "Joliet Manufacturing Company" https://archives.library.illinois.edu/archon/?p=creators/creator&id=1785, 6/4/2017.

27. http://www.encyclopedia.chicagohistory.org/pages/962.html "Demography: Chicago as a modern world city" Walter Nugent, The Electronic Encyclopedia of Chicago 2005 Chicago Historical Society.The Encyclopedia of Chicago © 2004 the Newberry Library. 10/12/2010.

28. "Iron and Steel" http://www.encyclopedia.chicagohistory.org/pages/653.html ; The Electronic Encyclopedia of Chicago © 2005 Chicago Historical Society. The Encyclopedia of Chicago © 2004 The Newberry Library. David Bensman and Mark R. Wilson. 10/12/2010.

29. "Joliet Iron and Steel Works," http://en.wikipedia.org/wiki/Joliet_Iron_and_Steel_Works, 10815/2010.

30. *Industrial Revolution in America*: Iron and Steel, ed by Kevin Hillstrom, Santa Barbara, Calif.: ABC-CLIO, c2005-2007. "Lives of the Workforce," by Jeffrey J. Hill, p 97-113., p.101.

31. Reef, Catherine. *Working in America: An Eyewitness History*. New York: Facts on File, 2000, p. 129.

32. *Industrial Revolution in America: Iron and Steel*, ed by Kevin Hillstrom, Santa Barbara, Calif.: ABC-CLIO, c2005-2007. "Lives of the Workforce," by Jeffrey J. Hill, p 97-113. P. 99.

33. Rasenberger, Jim. *America, 1908: the dawn of flight, the race to the Pole, the invention of the Model T, and the making of a modern nation*. New York: Scribner, 2007, p. 25.

34. Alexander, June Granatir, *Daily life in immigrant America, 1870-1920: how the second great wave of immigrants made their way in America*, Chi-

cago: Ivan R. Dee, c2009, p. 111.

35. "Iron and Steel" http://www.encyclopedia.chicagohistory.org/pages/653.html ; The Electronic Encyclopedia of Chicago © 2005 Chicago Historical Society. The Encyclopedia of Chicago, 2004 the Newberry Library. David Bensman and Mark R. Wilson.

36. http://www.canalcor.org/CCA2005/hist_Sign.html "National Significance of the I&N Canal," Canal Corridor Association 12/15/2010

37. Lamb, John. "Joliet Limestone: The Rise and Fall of a Nineteenth Century Building Material and Its Architectural Impact on the Joliet, Illinois Area." Quarterly Publication. Lockport, Ill.: Will County Historical Society, Winter 1997. https://www.lewisu.edu/imcanal/JohnLamb/section_46.pdf, p. 269-272.

38. http://www.canalcor.org/CCA2005/hist_Sign.html "National Significance of the I&N Canal," Canal Corridor Association 12/15/2010.

39. *Report of the canal commissioners of the state of Illinois to Governor Charles S. Deneen.* Springfield, Ill.: [Illinois Journal Printing Office], 1912, p. 14 ttps://archive.org/stream/reportofcanalcom1911illi/reportofcanalcom1911illi_djvu.txt; Uploaded by associate-alicia-schofield@archive.org on 10/17/2012; Digitized by the Internet Archive in 2012 with funding from University of Illinois Urbana-Champaign, 4/26/2017

Chapter 4: Starting From Scratch

1. *The Annals of Kansas 1886-1925 in 2 volumes v 2 1911-1925*, Mecham, Kirk, ed, Topeka, KS: Kansas State Historical Society, 1956, p. 149.

2. "News from Copeland" *The Montezuma Press*, June 19, 1919, p. 8.

3. "Local News." *The Jacksonian*, August 25, 1910, p. 6.

4. "Homestead News." *The Jacksonian*, July 1, 1917, p. 5.

Chapter 5: The Great War, the Flu, and a Dare

1. Casey, Jonathan. "Training in Kansas for a World War: Camp Funston in Photographs." *Kansas History - Autumn 2006*, Vol. 29, No. 3. p. 164-171.

2. "Thursday an Exciting Day," *The Montezuma Press*, April 18, 1918, p. 1.

3. Ibid.

4. "Will buy bonds," *The Montezuma Press*, April 25, 1918, p. 1.

5. Mecham, Kirk, ed. *The Annals of Kansas 1886-1925 in 2 volumes, v.2, 1911-1925.* Topeka, KS: Kansas State Historical Society, 1956, p. 207, 213

6. Ibid, p. 152

7. http://www.ers.usda.gov/data/wheat/yearbook/WheatYearbookTables-Full.pdf United States Department of Agriculture Economic Research Service; Domestic and International Prices Table 18, Wheat, average price received by farmers, United States, dollars per bushel, last updated 8/21/13

8. "Two Casulties," [sic] *The Montezuma Press*, September 5, 1918, v5, no 27, p. 1.

9. Casey, Jonathan. "Training in Kansas for a World War: Camp Funston in Photographs." *Kansas History - Autumn 2006*(Vol. 29, No. 3 p. 164-171)

10. Anton Erkoreka "Origins of the Spanish Influenza Pandemic (1918-1920) and its elation to the First World War. 1918-1920. *Journal of Molecular and Genetic Medicine,* November 30, 2009, https://www.ncbi.nlm.nih.gov/pmc/articles/PMC2805838/ February 4, 2018.

11. Carroll, Andrew. *Here is where: discovering America's great forgotten history.* Crown Archetype, 2013, p. 324.

12. A Canadian naturalist: musings on nature, history and anthropology; A-Z of Weird Animals: Part II—Influenza and You (And the Spanish flu, too http://acanadiannaturalist.net/2012/12/06/influenza-part-ii-a-rural-doctor-and-the-roots-of-the-spanish-flu/, 9/14/2013.

13. Carroll, Andrew. *Here is where: discovering America's great forgotten history.* Crown Archetype, 2013, p. 326.

14. http://www.twoop.com/medicine/archives/2005/10/1918_spanish_flu.html, 2005-2006 TWOOP Timelines "1918 Spanish Flu Timeline" 9/14/2013.

15. http://www.kshs.org/p/cool-things-influenza-sign/10369 Kansas State Historical Society Kansapedia "Cool Things-Influenza Sign" by Rebecca Mar-

tin.

16. "Camp Funston and Fort Riley clippings" v 2, K940.9 F96 p. 22 Kansas State Historical Society.

17. "Schools re-open," *The Montezuma Press*, January 2, 1919, p. 1.

18. "High School Notes," *The Montezuma Press*, March 27, 1919, p. 1.

19. *Annals of Kansas 1886-1925 in 2 volumes*, v 2 1911-1925, p275.

20. *Camp Funston Photograms*. K355 R45, v.4, n.9 Kansas State Historical Society.

21. http://www.flutrackers.com/forum/showthread.php?p=92146 "Life at Camp Funston: Reflections of Army Sergeant Charles L Johnson" Flu Trackers.Com Inc., 3/14/2008.

22. http://camp-john-wise-aerostation.com/ Camp John Wise Aerostation "Camp John Wise San Antonio Texas" by Richard DesChenes, 2/14/2008.

23. Ibid.

24. "Safe in theater, he misses show." *Stars and Stripes France*, Friday, March 29, 1918, 8.

25. http://www.worldwar1.com/dbc/balloon43.htm Doughboy Center: the Story of the American Expeditionary Forces presented by World War I.com "Camp John Wise, Texas" by Richard DesChenes 4/14/2008

26. Kendall Curlee, "GOLDBECK, EUGENE OMAR," *Handbook of Texas Online* (http://www.tshaonline.org/handbook/online/articles/fg049), accessed August 08, 2011. Uploaded on June 15, 2010. Published by the Texas State Historical Association.

27. National World War I Museum at Liberty Memorial, 100 W. 26th Street, Kansas City, MO 64108,

28. "Letters from Soldiers," *The Montezuma Press*, April 10, 1919, p. 1.

Chapter 6: To Kansas from the South

1 "All Around." *The Kansas Chief*. (Troy, Kansas), Thursday, January 27, 1921, p. 2

2. Stockwell, Roy. *John Graves (1703-1804) and his descendants*, Kansas City, Mo.: unknown, 1954, 251 pgs., p.1.

3. Hill, Heidi, contributor, "East Tennessee homes not entirely 'plantations.'" *The Daily Beacon*, February 2, 2015. http://utdailybeacon.com/news/2015/feb/2/east-tenn-historic-homes-not-entirely-plantations/. 2/8/2015.

4. "East Tennessee." *Tennessee in the American Civil War*, "http://en.wikipedia.org/wiki/Tennessee_in_the_American_Civil_War , 5/25/2012.

5. Dykeman, Wilma. *Tennessee: A Bicentennial History*, W.W. Norton and Company, Inc. New York, 1975, p.80.

6. East Tennessee "Antebellum Period," http://en.wikipedia.org/wiki/East_Tennessee. 5/25/2012.

7. Goodstein, Anita, "Slavery," *The East Tennessee Encyclopedia of History and Culture*. http://tennesseeencyclopedia.net/entry.php?rec=1211 , 5/20/2012.

8. Finke, Gene. *Yesterday and Today: Explorations in American History* "The Platte Purchase: First Overthrow of the Missouri Compromise," http://www.yandtblog.com/?p=118, 2/15/13.

9. Werner, Morris W. "Mosquito Creek Settlement, Doniphan County, Kansas," Kansas Heritage Group. www.kansasheritage.org/werner/mosquito.html, 1/28/2013.

10. Finke, Gene. *Yesterday and Today: Explorations in American History* "The Platte Purchase: First Overthrow of the Missouri Compromise," http://www.yandtblog.com/?p=118, 2/15/13.

11. Werner, Morris W. "Mosquito Creek Settlement, Doniphan County, Kansas," Kansas Heritage Group. www.kansasheritage.org/werner/mosquito.html, 1/28/2013.

12. "Abraham Lincoln in Doniphan County" *The Kansas Chief*, December 3, 1959, p. 1.

13. Lich, Glen E. "Forty Eighters" Texas State Historical Association: The Handbook of Texas http://www.tshaonline.org/handbook/online/articles/pnf01, 10/8/13.

14. Corbin, Joyce. "Abraham Lincoln in Kansas," Kansapedia—Kansas State Historical Society, http://www.kshs.org/kansapedia/abraham-lin-

coln-in-kansas/12132, 2/23/13.

15. Brinkerhoff, Fred W. "The Kansas Tour of Lincoln the Candidate." *Kansas History: Journal of the Great Plains, v31*, #4, Winter 2008-2009, p. 286.

16. Corbin, Joyce. "Abraham Lincoln in Kansas," Kansapedia—Kansas State Historical Society, http://www.kshs.org/kansapedia/abraham-lincoln-in-kansas/12132, 2/23/13.

17. "Wathena Boy Awarded Congressional Medal." *The Atchison Daily Globe*, Wednesday, February 20, 1946, p. 8.

18. "Abraham Lincoln in Doniphan County." *The Kansas Chief*, December 3, 1959, p. 1.

19: "Julia Parrett," email from Susan Ingels, susaningels@gmail.com April 3, 2012.

20. Ibid.

21. Ibid.

22. "Cocke County Tennessee, History and Topography," *Goodspeed's history of Tennessee (1887) and the Encyclopedia of Tennessee History*. http://www.tngenweb.org/cocke/cockehistandtopo.htm. 2/1/2012.

23. Whiteaker, Larry H. "Civil War" *The Tennessee Encyclopedia of History and Culture*. http://tennesseeencyclopedia.net/entry.php?rec=265. Tennessee Technological University, December 25, 2009, updated Jan 1, 2010; 1/15/2012

24. Ibid.

25. "Local and personal." *The Kansas Chief*," Thursday, November 28, 1912, p. 5.

26. "Troy Wins Again." *The Kansas Chief*," Thursday, January 23, 1913, p. 1

27. "All around." *The Kansas Chief*," Thursday, February 15, 1917, p. 3.

28. "High School Notes." *The Kansas Chief*," Thursday, February 22, 1917, p. 1.

Chapter 7: The Family Begins to Grow

1. "Married." *The Montezuma Press*, June 21, 1921, p. 4

2. "Local Mention," *The Montezuma Press*, December 15, 1921, p. 3.

3. *The Montezuma Press*, April 28, 1921, p. 2.

4. The Montezuma Press, May 5, 1921, p. 4..

5. "Card of Thanks," *The Montezuma Press*, Thursday, May 14, 1923, p. 8.

6. Lamb, John. Lockport, *Illinois: The Old Canal Town*. Charleston, SC: Arcadia Publishing, 1999, p.73

7. "Notice." *The Montezuma Press*, April 24, 1924, p.1.

8. "Notice." *The Montezuma Press*, May 29, 1924, p. 1.

9. "Some Fine Celery," *The Montezuma Press*, September 20, 1934, p. 1.

10. "50th Wedding Anniversary," *The Montezuma Press*, November 28, 1940, p. 1.

11. "O.R. Winkler Passes Away Saturday," *The Montezuma Press*, March 20, 1941, p.1.

Chapter 8: Harvesting Wheat and Dust

1. Saul, Norman E. "Myth and History: Turkey Red Wheat and the `Kansas Miracle'." *Heritage of the Great Plains 22* (Summer 1989): 1-13., p. 4.

2. "Bernhard Warkentin and the Making of the Wheat State." Saul, Norman E. *John Brown to Bob Dole: Movers and Shakers in Kansas History*, ed by Virgil W. Dean, University Press of Kansas, 2006, p. 110.

3. "Myth and History" p. 7.

4. Ibid, p. 7.

5. Ibid, p. 8.

6. http://memory.loc.gov/ammem/award97/ndfahtml/ngp_farm_threshing.html The Library of Congress American Memory, http://memory.loc.gov/ammem/award97/ndfahtml/ngphome.htmlNorthern Great Plains: Photographs from the Fred Hultstrand and F.A. Pazandak Collections Northern Great

Plains, 1880-1920, F.A. Pazandak, Farming the Land; Implements Used on the Farm "Threshing Machine"; 9/22/2013

7. http://drought.unl.edu/DroughtBasics/DustBowl/RainFollowsthePlow.aspx National Drought Mitigation Center, Drought Basics "Rain Follows the Plow"; 9/22/2013

8. Luther, F.M., and sons. "Two Stories." 1911. TS. C338 .109781 F679tw Western History (Conservation, Tenth Mountain Division) Collection, the Denver Public Library. [p.5]

9. Unruh, Inez. The Day I Ran Over Ruby & Frank. Phoenix Publishing Group, Phoenix, 2000, p.11.

10. Sandler, Martin W. *The Dust Bowl through the Lens: How Photography Revealed and Helped Remedy a National Disaster*. New York: Walker and Co, 2009, p. 22

11. Yancey, Diane, *Life during the Dust Bowl*, San Diego: Lucent Books, 2004, p. 12.

12. Ibid, p. 56.

Chapter 9: Mining Boom and Bust

1. Cool Things - Mining Town Minerals, Kansas State Historical Society, http://www.kshs.org/kansapedia/cool-things-mining-town-minerals/15118 Date Created: January 2010 Date Modified: March 201 10/26/2014

2: Brosius, Liz, and Sawin, Robert S. "Lead and Zinc Mining in Kansas," Kansas Geologic Survey, Public Information Circular (PIC) 17, http://www.kgs.ku.edu/Publications/pic17/pic17_2.html 10/26/14.

3. Ibid.

4. Brady, Lawrence. "Mining History in Kansas," U.S. Department of Transportation, Federal Highway Administration, Geotechnical Engineering, Interstate Technical Group on abandoned Underground Mines Third Biennial Workshop. http://www.fhwa.dot.gov/engineering/geotech/hazards/mine/workshops/kdot/kansas01.cfm, 9/22/2013.

5. "Died From Mine Accident." *The Columbus Daily Advocate*, Columbus, Kansas, Saturday, May 15, 1915, p. 1.

6. An email from Linda Kennedy, heritagectr@embargmail.com, Baxter Springs Heritage Center, 11/4/14.

7. Rosner, David, and Markowitz, Gerald E. *Deadly Dust: Silicosis and the on-going struggle to protect worker's health, new and expanded edition*, University of Michigan Press, 2005, p. 145.

8. An mail from Linda Kennedy, heritagectr@embargmail.com, Baxter Springs Heritage Center, 11/4/14.

9. Rosner, David, and Markowitz, Gerald E. *Deadly Dust: Silicosis and the on-going struggle to protect worker's health, new and expanded edition*, University of Michigan Press, 2005, p. 145.

10. Weiser, Kathy. "Legends of America, Galena, Kansas," http://www.legendsofamerica.com/ks-galena2.html, p. 2, updated June 2010; 9/22/2013.

11. "Population of cities in Kansas, 1900-2010." www.ipsr.ku.edu/ksdata/ksah/population/2pop33.pdf 10/24/14

12. *Live Cherokee County*, v 1, August 2012, p. 6; Machelle Smith, Editor, www.livecherokeecounty.com

13. Suggs, George G. *Union Busting in the Tri-State: The Oklahoma, Kansas, and Missouri Metal Workers' Strike of 1935.* Norman: University of Oklahoma Press, 1986, p. 22.

14. http://pumpedupkicksonroute66.com/Websites/Route66/Joplin_Globe_6_29_35.pdf "Route 66: Pumped up Kicks on Route 66—Day 10: Joplin to Galena" 11/2/14.

15. Ibid.

16. Ford, Susan. "World War II Airbases in Kansas." *Kansas Preservation*. v34, n4, p. 4 http://www.kshs.org/resource/ks_preservation/2012v34n4.pdf, 11/15/14

17. "Dodge City Army Airfield" http://en.wikipedia.org/wiki/Dodge_City_Army_Airfield Wikipedia, last modified April 2, 2013, 9/22/2013

18. "Squadron News." *Boot Hill Marauder.* Dodge City, Ks, Feb 24, 1945, p. 3,

Chapter 10: Another Generation Begins

1. Kansas Historical Society. Kansapedia. "Angell Plow." https://www.kshs.org/kansapedia/angell-plow/10136. Last modified July 2017. 9/4/2017.

Chapter 13: From Heat and Dust to Floods and Blizzards

1. "The 1951 Kansas - Missouri Floods ... Have We Forgotten?" http://www.crh.noaa.gov/mbrfc/flood51.pdf 12/1/2014.

2. "The 1951 Floods in Kansas Revisited" United States Geological Survey Kansas Water Science center, USGS Fact Sheet 041-01 May 2001 http://ks.water.usgs.gov/pubs/fact-sheets/fs.041-01.html 12/1/2014 .

3. Luther, F.M., and sons. "Two Stories." 1911. TS. C338 .109781 F679tw Western History (Conservation, Tenth Mountain Division) Collection, the Denver Public Library. [p.5].

4. "Lights turned on", *The Montezuma Press*, December 15, 1921, p.1.

5. "Rural electrification" Kansas Historical Society, December, 2004, modified March 2013, http://www.kshs.org/p/kansas-historical-markers/14999#b, 10/6/2013

6. "Rural electrification" http://www.kshs.org/p/kansas-historical-markers/14999#b, 10/6/2013.

7. "Fruehauf, Erich. "Fifty years on a one-family farm in central Kansas." (Second Installment) *Kansas History, A Journal of the Central Plains*, Winter, 1979, volume 2, number 4, Kansas State Historical Society, Forrest R. Blackburn managing editor, p. 258.

Chapter 17: Up and Down the Hill

1. http://www.legendsofamerica.com/na-kiowa.html Legends of America, "Native American Legends-Kiowa: Nomadic Warriors of the Plains" Kathy Weiser, updated July 2010; 9/22/13.

2. http://www.cimarronkansas.net/elsiewagner1.htm#6 Cimarron Kansas Network, "Cimarron: the Growth of a Town—Hostile Indians" by Elsie D. Wagner 1976; 9/22/2013.

Chapter 18: Off to School by Horse and Bus

1. Samuelson, Bill. *The One Room Country Schools of Kansas*, Chester Press, Emporia, 1995 p. 54.

2. Homestead School 1909-1941 District 20, author unknown. [p.1].

3. *The One Room Country Schools of Kansas*, p. 64.

4. Homestead School 1909-1941 District 20, author unknown. [p.16].

5. *The One Room Country Schools of Kansas*, p. 196

6. *The One Room Country Schools of Kansas*, p. 170.

7. McNabb, Bridget. "Match Made in Kansas." Kansas. Winter 2014, vol 70, issue 4, p. 47.

www.ingramcontent.com/pod-product-compliance
Lightning Source LLC
Chambersburg PA
CBHW021945290426
44108CB00012B/966